THE FINE LINE

THE FINE LINE

Re-envisioning the Gap
between **Christ** and **Culture**

KARY OBERBRUNNER

ZONDERVAN®

ZONDERVAN.com/
AUTHORTRACKER
follow your favorite authors

The Fine Line
Copyright © 2008 by Kary Oberbrunner

This title is also available in a Zondervan audio edition. Visit *www.zondervan.fm.*

Requests for information should be addressed to:

Zondervan, *Grand Rapids, Michigan* 49530

Library of Congress Cataloging-in-Publication Data

Oberbrunner, Kary, 1976–
    The fine line : re-envisioning Christ and culture / Kary Oberbrunner.
       p.   cm.
    Includes bibliographical references and index.
    ISBN 978-0-310-28545-8 (softcover : alk. paper)
    1. Christianity and culture. I. Title.
  BR115.C8O24 2009
  261—dc22   2008033319

Interior design by Beth Shagene

Printed in the United States of America

08 09 10 11 12 13 14 • 23 22 21 20 19 18 17 16 15 14 13 12 11 10 9 8 7 6 5 4 3 2 1

For Isabel
You've captured my heart.

CONTENTS

Religion is for those who don't want to go to Hell.
Spirituality is for those of us who have already been through it.
Anonymous

A NOTE
TO THE READER

We all have a context—a history, some might call it. The book you're about to read and the author who wrote it are no exception.

First, the book.

Over fifty years ago Yale professor H. Richard Niebuhr published a seminal book. When *Christ and Culture* was released, it rocked the church and the world. Niebuhr's work, regarded as "one of the most vital books of our time,"[1] has dominated the conversation for nearly six decades. For many Christians the book scratched their itch about how to live in the world but not of the world. Niebuhr proved to be the voice for his generation and then some. His five models for understanding a Christian's role in culture are still discussed and debated in the halls of academia today.

Although Niebuhr and his models are still worthy, our world has changed. Now it's time for our generation to re-envision what it means to live in the world but not be of the world. We need to unravel the fine line and discover how to be committed to both our Christianity and our culture. And so this book presents a new model for a new generation.

If you're reading this book within the context of a group, I invite you to interact with the discussion questions at the end of the book. My guess is that they'll keep the conversation flowing.

Now, the author part.

I tell people I'm a professional Christian. Don't be too impressed. It just means I'm a pastor. I've served at Grace Church in Powell, Ohio, for the last seven years, and I've done pretty much everything there, including donating my old Dodge Spirit to be smashed on the last night of youth group. The things we justify in the name of outreach.

I'm not exempt from the irrelevant tendencies I discuss in the book. In fact, I know some of them all too well. Still, both I and the people I run with strive to live as Transformists. We long to be a community of faith that discovers the fine line and then camps right smack in the middle of this sophisticated paradox. My guess is that this is your longing too.

I'll look for you there.

THE PHONE IS RINGING

Skating rinks.

Who doesn't love these wonderful, wretched institutions? I think I started and ended more middle school "relationships" there than I care to remember.

The distinct sound of the air hockey puck smacking against the table, the smell of buttery popcorn at the snack bar, and the feel of those worn tan skates with bright orange wheels—these memories define my early adolescent years.

Of course, my parents allowed me to attend only "Christian" skate nights. My virgin ears weren't allowed to hear the likes of Madonna or Color Me Badd. But even these sanctified skate nights had their limits. Every Thursday at the stroke of nine, the disc jockey switched the music from Christian back to secular. That's when my friends and I had better be out of the building or else we would promptly turn into pumpkins.

For some reason on one particular night I lingered past the safety of 9:00 p.m. Maybe my laces got tangled. Maybe my friend's mom forgot to pick us up.

I can't remember.

What I do remember are the lyrics from that one song, that

"secular" song: "That's me in the corner, that's me in the spotlight, losing my religion."

I felt like Judas when I heard it, like I was betraying the faith. Although the song sounded irreligious, I couldn't deny that something about the plaintive voice coming through the speakers at the skating rink that night resonated with me. The song put words to feelings lodged deep within me. Whether the band R.E.M. intended it or not, I viewed the song as a type of psalm boldly declaring doubts and concerns.

I didn't know much about the band at the time, but an entire generation latched on to that song, evidenced by the fact that in 1991, R.E.M. won a Grammy Award for Best Pop Performance and "Losing My Religion" is listed as #169 on *Rolling Stone*'s five hundred greatest songs of all time.

All I knew was that lead singer Michael Stipe had a unique voice and R.E.M. a unique sound, at least compared to the Christian songs popular during the early nineties. I think Michael W. Smith's "crossover" song "Place in This World" was about as edgy as things got back then.

Stipe's haunting voice and penetrating lyrics stuck with me for months, re-creating in me the same side effect I feel when I eat one too many barbecue ribs at summer cookouts: heavy and lethargic—no touch football after lunch.

Odd, isn't it? Here I was an eighth grader caught somewhere between two songs, echoing the cries of two Michaels. At that time in my life, I often prayed to God that he would show me *my place in this world* while feeling that I was *losing my religion.*

Sometimes things don't change much.

Fast-forward a whole bunch of years and I am still caught between the same two songs. I'm still waiting for the angst to end. I know Jesus and I love Jesus more today than I did back in that skating rink many years ago, but today it seems as though I have more questions about Christianity than answers.

I'm not happy about my angst. And if it were possible, I wish I could go back to a time when everything was black and white and simple, to the time when life was easily categorized like the music in the skating rink: Christian or secular. I think back to that time, somewhere in my childhood, when making Bible characters out of Popsicle sticks was about as complicated as life got.

Even though I'm thirty-one, I'm still trying to find my place in this world. Shouldn't I know by now what I want to be when I grow up?

But it's bigger than simply what I want to do in the future. It's also about how I should live now. I want to be relevant to the world, to impact it, and maybe even transform it. At the same time, I don't want to look just like the world looks.

This tension isn't unique to middle school skaters. It's the unavoidable tension that exists for each of us who believe in the God of the Bible. Jesus addressed this tension when he instructed his followers about their relationship with the world. He told them to be *in* the world but not *of* it.

As if that makes things a whole lot clearer. Or easier.

One thing is certain: there's a fine line between *in* and *of.* In my life I've tried to avoid this tension; I've pretended this fine line doesn't exist. But pretending doesn't make the tension go away. It only makes *us* go away—one more irrelevant Christian.

I'm pretty sure this tension that's been with me from childhood until now isn't going away anytime soon. Discovering the fine line between *in the world* and *of the world* isn't easy, but I have to try. I don't want to be caught living a lie—or manufacturing one. If you're like me, then you're willing to explore this tension and you're willing to pay the cost of living with this tension.

At certain times throughout history, Christians avoided the

tension and, as we'll see in our story, the church and the world suffered because of it. Living a lie prevents people from living free.

At other times, people ventured into the unknown and celebrated the mystery instead of suppressing it. Within the process, some lost their religion. Others not only found their place in the world but, more importantly, they found Jesus.

In my life there have been a few times when things took a big turn. Most of the time these turns were quite unexpected. You could even say they happened on ordinary days.

One time it happened after my wife, Kelly, took a pregnancy test. Her giddy smile left me in a daze for a couple days. Another time it happened after I opened the mailbox. The letter confirmed the military's rejection of me serving as a chaplain. And still another time it happened through a phone call. I was offered a new position in a new state. Five months later we arrived in Columbus, Ohio, and began driving down different roads, shopping at a different grocery store, and breathing in a different neighbor's smoke through our apartment vents.

Although these big changes happened in a variety of ways, one thing was similar in every case: these changes all started with dialogue.

> The little plastic pregnancy test spoke. We shouted.
> The letter from the military offered condolences. I cried.
> And the last: the phone rang. I picked it up.

Remember that chilling scene in *The Matrix* when Neo, played by Keanu Reeves, receives an unexpected package on a very ordinary day? He gingerly opens the flap and a cell phone slides into his hand. Immediately, it starts to ring. He has a hunch about the purpose of the call. It concerns the explanation of the Matrix. But now Neo has a choice. Will he answer the phone or ignore the call? If he enters into the dialogue, his predictable life will be forever changed.

And so it is with this story—it's a kind of call too. But it's about something more complicated than even the Matrix. It's about living *in* the world without being *of* the world. It's about the tension we must live with and fight through. It's about "the fine line."

Now that you've gingerly opened this book, you too have a choice.

The phone is ringing. Will you answer it?

PART I

THE BATTLE LINES

It is well that war is so terrible—
otherwise we would grow too fond of it.
Robert E. Lee

CHAPTER 1

WALKING THE LINE

Ask anyone who's single: there's a fine line between friendly and flirtatious.

Ask any athlete: there's a fine line between confidence and arrogance.

Ask any Christ-follower: there's a fine line between being *in* the world and being *of* the world.

The danger of walking the line is that we may accidentally cross it — wherever the line is. This fear often makes us shrink back and fall prey to the other extreme and become, in the case of the single, shy; the athlete, timid; and the believer, irrelevant.

Then what?

People miss out on having healthy friendships. Fans miss out on celebrating victories with their team. And the world misses out on seeing the kingdom of God on earth.

Discovering this fine line is difficult but not impossible. All who follow Jesus must wrestle with this question and emerge with some kind of answer. This question of relevance, as author and journalist Michael Joseph Gross put it, is "the most basic ethical question of the Christian faith."[1]

I've seen enough of the next generation leaving the church.

According to some estimates, 58 percent of young adults who attended church at eighteen no longer attend by age twenty-nine. This number accounts for more than eight million twentysomethings who are simply "missing in action."[2]

Why are so many from this generation voting on spiritual matters with their absence?

Perhaps it has something to do with the fact that there is little difference between the attitudes and actions of believers and unbelievers. Rather than drawing people to Christ, many Christians are pushing people away because of the disconnection between what we say and how we live.

That cannot continue.

Christ-followers are supposed to be the most liberated, grace-filled people on earth. We're supposed to have what people want — a message so powerful it will cause the dead to rise and the blind to see. We're supposed to have the living God living inside us. We're supposed to know how to live in the world but not be of it.

Most believers I know *don't* know. Most are either living *out* of the world or they're *of* the world. No wonder Christians have so little impact, so little relevance. Now more than ever, we need to understand how to live in the world but not be of it.

And that's exactly what this book will do: help you discover the fine line.

CHAPTER 2

DIVIDED WE FALL

Lately I've been guilty of an admittedly nerdy behavior.

I've been checking out documentaries from my local library. I'm easily swayed by free, so I've been consuming documentaries on civil rights, Martin Luther King Jr., and JFK. Being a child of the eighties and nineties, I had never witnessed a divided country.

Something fierce was brewing in the 1960s, and our country was falling apart. Dogs and fire hoses were used to attack civil rights protesters in the South while activists battled for a world without segregation. James Meredith, the first African American to attend the University of Mississippi, required an escort of federal marshals to protect him because his life was threatened. Our country was devouring itself, and for a time it appeared there wasn't much anyone could do about it.

Finally some people realized they could change reality if they worked together. This remnant, comprised of both blacks and whites, believed in the possibility of a different way and a different world. Marches, rallies, and sit-ins tangibly announced that something was deeply wrong with the world as they knew it. And slowly their world began to change.

I fear today's church is in a similar predicament: there's a war that's brewing and no end is in sight. Sadly, the church of Jesus Christ is at war with itself. Whether speaking of a country divided over racism or a church divided over relevance, Jesus' words, and then much later Abraham Lincoln's, are true: "If a house is divided against itself, that house cannot stand" (Mark 3:25).

Choosing Sides

The church has divided itself and reassembled into two main camps that at best tolerate one another. If we're honest we'll admit that these two groups are far from the kind of evangelism Jesus commanded when he said, "By this everyone will know that you are my disciples, if you love one another" (John 13:35 TNIV). Many within these camps detest those in the other camp. They might not admit it, but the enmity surfaces in casual comments that reflect deep feelings.

The first camp separates itself from people, society, and culture in order to stay "unstained." They turn God's commands, plus hundreds of other rules and laws, into a heavy burden that supposedly grants personal holiness (see 1 John 5:3). They judge others in light of their self-made religion. They're laced with fear: fear of sinning, fear of compromising, fear of enjoying anything. These people make up the Separatist camp.

The second camp conforms itself to the ideals and philosophies of the world. They value what the world values and worship what it worships. They're a cookie-cutter cutout of pop culture. Attempting to be all things to all people and to enjoy what God has created, they engage in ungodly activity. Flaunting their freedom, they condemn Separatists for their disciplined lifestyle. These people make up the Conformist camp.

Whatever the merits of each camp, the unfortunate truth is that both have become irrelevant, though for very different reasons. Self-deceived Separatists justify their behavior because of their perceived love for God. Self-deceived Conformists justify their behavior because of their perceived love for people. But it isn't love that characterizes either camp, as Jesus commands, but unbalance. And the church and the world both suffer because of it.

Just as civil rights campaigners changed the face of America, a remnant of Christians discontented with the state of the church are beginning to change things. Recovering Separatists and recovering Conformists are partnering together because they believe in a different way and a different world. This new group of Christians, a group I call Transformists, are learning to balance Christianity and culture, loving God and loving people. These Transformists are arising with a steady force.

In 1858, the United States was fractured, split right down the middle over the issue of slavery. People chose sides and dug in their heels. Something had to be done, but what? Would the solution be found through war, protest, or politics? And if through politics, who would be the leader?

That year, when Illinois Republican delegates met in the statehouse in Springfield for their state convention, they chose Abraham Lincoln as their candidate for the US Senate, hoping to unseat Democrat Stephen A. Douglas. A few hours later, Lincoln kicked off his bid for the Senate with an address to his Republican colleagues that would come to be known as the "House Divided" speech.

Mr. President and Gentlemen of the Convention:

If we could first know where we are and whither we are tending, we could better judge what to do and how to do it. We are now far into the fifth year since a policy was initiated with the avowed object and confident promise of putting an end to slavery agitation. Under the operation of that policy, that agitation has not only not ceased but has constantly augmented. In my opinion, it will not cease until a crisis shall have been reached and passed. "A house divided against itself cannot stand." I believe this government cannot endure, permanently, half slave and half free. I do not expect the Union to be dissolved; I do not expect the house to fall; but I do expect it will cease to be divided. It will become all one thing, or all the other.[1]

Lincoln knew the country couldn't continue in its current state of fracture. Something would eventually give. And though many disagreed profoundly with him, he proposed a strategy to navigate through the crisis. He told his colleagues and the country that they must answer three questions: Where are we? What should we do? How do we do it?

Eventually the country answered these questions, though it was a difficult and bloody process. The cost was significant, but the change was essential. After many years, the country emerged stronger and, more importantly, unified.

Our Three Questions

If the church ever hopes to wake from its slumber of irrelevance, if it longs to turn its focus outward, away from the internal war between the Separatists and Conformists, then three questions must be answered. These three questions will help the church in its current crisis just as they helped America over a century ago.

The church, defined in the Scriptures as the household of God, is also divided, fractured down the middle. People have chosen sides and dug in their heels. The divisive issue is how to be in the world, not of it. Something has to be done, but what? Nothing can change until we, like antebellum America, answer three questions:

Where are we?

What should we do?

How do we do it?

Where Are We?

I rarely go to the mall. It isn't that I don't like shopping, it's that I'm scared I'll get lost. I beeline for the map kiosk, searching for those comforting words: You Are Here. I can't move unless I know where I am. I can try, but without a reference point, I'll be stuck in the mall all afternoon — a scary thought indeed.

Similarly, the church can't move toward relevance until we first understand the irrelevance that resides deep within each one of us. Like the mall map, we need a reference point. We need the You Are Here arrow to point within our lives.

To find out where we are, we must first explore what it looks like to live in the world but not be of it. By doing so, we'll demystify what it means to live a life of relevance. Unfortunately, historically fuzzy thinking, initiated by Separatists and Conformists, has tended to dominate this dialogue.

Why?

Fuzzy thinking has its payoff. There's a kind of comfort in being unclear because we never know if we're missing the mark. Many Christ-followers talk as if they want to be relevant, but if they're honest, most aren't even sure what relevance is or if they want it once they know. If we ever hope to integrate our Christianity with our culture, we need to acknowledge this fuzziness and overcome it, which is what we will do in part 2. We'll encounter a biblical definition of relevance and a related paradigm that will demonstrate what it means to live in the world but not be of it. We'll uncover the specifics of the irrelevance deep inside us and why we often choose to live in less than ideal extremes.

What Should We Do?

Once we answer where we are, we can explore what we should do. We'll look, in part 3, at examples of people who lived in the world, but were not of it—people like the apostle Paul at Mars Hill. We'll not only look at his situation but also at his strategy.

We'll encounter several common obstacles that prevent us from living relevant lives. We'll discover that many of us have a shallow love for God because we've adopted a compartmentalized understanding of the world. We tend to break our lives down into categories like sacred and secular.

Also, because most of us love ourselves the wrong way, this section reveals the absurdity of thinking that loving our neighbors as ourselves is the easy answer for relevance. Although we tend to be selfish, we also live in an age in which more people abuse and even hate themselves. Self-help seminars are not the answer. We need more than behavioral changes; we need a radical change in our thinking. We need to see ourselves as God sees us and love ourselves as God loves us. Only then can we love others the right way and become relevant to the world around us.

How Do We Do It?

In part 4, we'll get even more practical. How exactly do we make these changes? We'll examine the factors that contribute to becoming a Transformist. We'll uncover how some people are able to transcend irrelevance. We'll explore the defining characteristics, habits, and disciplines of relevant people.

We'll meet Transformists like Mark, Jennifer, Amy, and Micah and see their courage as they inspire a community of faith called the Landing Place in the Short North, an artistic hub of Columbus, Ohio. We'll listen to John and Kori share their stories about confronting suffering by creating paths of hope for children otherwise headed into the sex slave industry in Asia.

In these chapters we'll examine why it's critical to invite the kingdom of God and embody it as a present reality in our everyday lives. Although the kingdom isn't yet here in its fullness, it's what Jesus taught and it's how Jesus lived. And when Jesus came to earth, he brought with him a brand-new set of principles to live by. Transformists orient their lives according to this new way of understanding the world.

We'll also explore why we must become "bilingual." Every good missionary knows the importance of speaking other languages. We'll learn to speak the same truth to different cultures and different worldviews. Transformists must be able to bridge the communication gap and live a culturally relevant life while maintaining a deep commitment to Christianity.

Answering these three questions will allow us to surface from the civil war that rages within the church and within our own hearts. It will take us to the crux of being in the world but not being of it— right to the fine line. And it is there that we'll make our stand.

PART II

WHERE ARE WE?

Not all who wander are lost.

J. R. R. Tolkien

CHAPTER 3

UNDER THE SUN

What if it turns out that the Separatist and Conformist camps are as old as the garden of Eden? Can that be true? If it is, how should we feel?

On one hand, we can feel relieved—we're not unique. We can look to others who have traveled before us and wrestled with the concept of relevance. Maybe we could even avoid their mistakes and emulate their successes.

On the other hand, we feel a little disappointed. The whole dialogue would lose some of its intrigue. What's innovative and sexy about discussing a topic as old as humanity?

Sexy or not, it's our job to wrestle with this question: What does it look like to live in the world but not be of it? Perhaps the innovation comes when each generation discovers its own successful strategies for answering that question.

Adam and Eve were the first to confront the question. And we have much to learn from their strategies, unsuccessful and ungodly as they were. Beginning in the garden of Eden, the battle lines were drawn, and, like the serpent, the Separatist and Conformist camps reared their ugly heads.

The Ancient Eden

You probably know the story. The first temptation involved, of all things, a tree.

> And the LORD God commanded the man, "You are free to eat from any tree in the garden; but you must not eat from the tree of the knowledge of good and evil, for when you eat of it you will surely die."
>
> Genesis 2:16–17

Some might see this story as a cruel set-up: Go ahead, Adam. Skip through paradise. Have fun. And even though I've created you immortal, I expect that for all of eternity you won't eat of the forbidden tree. That's all I ask. Can you do it?

Others might see the story as a generous gift: Adam, I've created all these things for you. The world is at your fingertips. There are orange trees and orangutans, roses and rivers, and, above all, perfect peace. Enjoy yourself. Explore. Relax in this paradise that meets all your desires. Because I care about you, and I don't want to see you hurt, I will warn you: There's one tree in the middle of the garden. Stay away from it. If you eat it you'll die.

Regardless of how you see the story, it's clear that temptations toward Separatism and Conformism emerged with intensity, whispering for Adam and Eve to disobey God's words.

I imagine myself in the garden. If I leaned toward the Conformist camp, I'd ignore God's word and head straight for the tree. Well, I might wait for a few hundred years, but I'd head toward it all the same. Of course, I wouldn't do so with the intention of eating the forbidden fruit. Instead, I'd justify my need to be near the tree in order to be "familiar" with it. Maybe I'd tell myself that I needed to study it in order to know why it would kill me. Perhaps I'd start to think that God was holding out on me, that he didn't have my best interest in mind. I might play a little game: get as close to the fruit as possible without actually eating it. As innocent as all these mental and spiritual gymnastics might sound, the result would still be the same. I'd eat the fruit and immediately experience death.

But if I leaned toward the Separatist camp, I'd do something entirely different.

I'd start by adding to God's words. God simply told me not to eat from that one tree. But that wouldn't be good enough. I'd add that I couldn't touch the fruit either; it's only common sense. And if I shouldn't touch it then I should build a fence around it too. Soon I'd give up eating fruit altogether, just in case it reminded me of the forbidden fruit. In spite of all these rules I would still lust after the fruit, but I sure wouldn't admit that. To deal with my lust, I'd create another rule that I couldn't talk to my wife just in case she were to mention the forbidden tree in conversation. Eventually, I'd get so frustrated with myself I'd just leave the garden in order not to struggle anymore. Of course, I could still think about it, even when I'm no longer in the garden.

Still, my rules would be so brilliant, at least on the outside, that I'd make my wife—and anyone else around—observe them. If they rejected my advice and touched the fruit, spoke about the fruit, or failed to help me build a fence around the fruit, then I'd condemn them and denounce them as less spiritual. Ironically, because of my excessive rules, I would have broken several of God's *positive* commands. If I'm no longer in the garden, then I can't enjoy eating from the other trees. And if I'm not talking to my wife, it's just that much more difficult to be fruitful, multiply, and fill the earth (see Genesis 1:28). Just stating the obvious.

The Original Irrelevant Ones

Eve was on the fast track of imitating my Separatist plan to avoid the forbidden fruit:

> The woman said to the serpent, "We may eat fruit from the trees
> in the garden, but God did say, 'You must not eat fruit from the
> tree that is in the middle of the garden, *and you must not touch it*,
> or you will die.'"
>
> Genesis 3:2–3, emphasis mine

Eve added that they couldn't touch the fruit either. Although it was probably a good idea not to touch it, the Bible never records that God commanded this. When we unpack her reply, some interesting things emerge. In her mind, God was more restrictive and limiting than he actually was. Classic Separatist behavior.

Adam, though, was the first Conformist. He could have resisted temptation and been a Transformist, one who obeys God's word. Although we're not told for how long, there was a period of time when Adam had not yet eaten the fruit after Eve had. Everyone else in the world (we're only talking about Eve here) gave in, and he had a choice not to conform. But you know the story. He ignored God's word and ate the forbidden fruit—he needed to be like everyone else. Typical Conformist behavior.

From the very beginning it seemed easier to separate or conform instead of transform—be in the world but not be of it. Eve tried to use her rules to get *out* of the world, and Adam, in accommodating, became *of* the world. They forfeited life on the fine line. They had three choices—only one of them relevant. But they settled for separatism, conformism, and, ultimately, irrelevance.

Our Eden

There are some haunting parallels between our situation and that of our forebears. In our day, "forbidden fruit" grows on our computer screens, ripens in our mouths when we gossip, and spoils in our overstocked refrigerators. We don't have one alluring tree—we have millions.

God told Adam and Eve not to eat from the tree. And God tells us not to be conformed to the world. God has desired something from the beginning. He wants his people to transform the culture they're in — to pattern themselves after him, not the world in which they live.

Why is God so passionate about his people being different from the world?

He wants us to point others to him, something that's impossible to do when we're consumed by the world. This was true for ancient Israel too. God wanted to transform that nation so it, in turn, could transform everything it contacted: people, land, kingdoms, nations, and religions. He wanted Israel to be a light in a dark place.

> It is too small a thing for you to be my servant
>> to restore the tribes of Jacob
>> and bring back those of Israel I have kept.
> I will also make you a light for the Gentiles,
>> that you may bring my salvation to the ends of the earth.
>
>   Isaiah 49:6

How does the world notice our light? Through our righteous acts. "Let your light shine before men in such a way that they may see your good works, and glorify your Father who is in heaven" (Matthew 5:16 NASB). Our difference from the world, not our similarity to it, sets us apart. But even though Christ-followers are called to be different, we're also called to transform the world. Here lies the tension. We can't be so far removed from the world that we lose contact, and we can't be so much like the world that we're no different from it.

Christ understood this dilemma, and walking this fine line was his strategy. He immersed himself in the world, but he was different from it. In his high priestly prayer, found in John 17, he prayed that we, his followers, would emulate his successful strategy.

My prayer is not that you take them out of the world but that you
protect them from the evil one. They are not of the world, even
as I am not of it. Sanctify them by the truth; your word is truth.
As you sent me into the world, I have sent them into the world.

John 17:15 – 18

Being in the world but not of it was God's call for the first humans,
beginning in the garden, and it's still Christ's call for his church.
Even though Adam and Eve chose Separatism and Conformism, we
don't have to. We have the Holy Spirit living inside us, enabling us
to be Transformists. We can choose to walk away from irrelevance,
but it isn't easy.

Our Irrelevant Extremes

When confronted with the countless types of fruit in our culture — whether forbidden or wholesome — most of us react poorly.
We see the fruit of culture — the variety, the options, the colors, the
flavors — and we despair of ever discerning bad from good. And the
Bible tells us that "everything created by God is good, and nothing is
to be rejected if it is received with gratitude" (1 Timothy 4:4 NASB).
But we also recognize the Bible has other things to say about the
fruit within the world. Some of it is dangerous and even deadly. What
are we to make of this paradox? There's a line somewhere. But how
do we know when we're walking the line and when we're tiptoeing
outside of it? Maybe it was easier for Adam and Eve with only one
bad tree.

Most of us do one of two things. If we're Separatists we reason
that since *some* fruit in the world is toxic, *all* should be avoided. The
risk of choosing wrong leads us to not choose anything at all, and so
we boycott culture rather than discern it. Instead, we create our own
Christian subculture, feeling safer in a place where other Christians
call the shots.

If we're Conformists, we reason that it's not worth the effort to discern between what's tolerable and what's toxic. We don't want to invest the energy because it takes too many brain cells. Instead, we end up consuming everything, regardless of its merit.

To the world, Separatists seem to be out of touch, opposed to everything for no good reason and motivated only by a desire to condemn others. Separatists are seen as quintessential judgers, narrow-minded and intolerant.

Conformists, on the other hand, seem to be exactly the same as the world. The world fails to notice anything positive or spiritual about Conformists because it's hidden beneath sinful, carnal lifestyle choices. Conformists are just one more splinter group in a materialistic, empty world.

Transformists live on the fine line and battle to integrate their Christianity with their culture. This camp causes critics to freeze in their tracks and rethink the only stereotypes of Christians they know. Transformists cause the world to stop, stare, and shut up, exactly what God intends. "For such is the will of God that by doing right you may silence the ignorance of foolish men" (1 Peter 2:15 NASB).

The only way we can change stereotypes is to change ourselves. And the only way to change ourselves is to follow Jesus and allow him to change us.

This too is nothing new, but it is, nevertheless, our charge.

CHAPTER 4

THE ANCIENT DONKEY

Jesus knew the question—Who is my neighbor?—was a set-up, but he answered it anyway. Some questions can't be answered with a statement—they need a story. So Jesus told one.

We'll get to his story in a moment, but first here's one of mine.

The New Buzzword

A couple years ago I sat down with a dean of a seminary in the Midwest. He explained that his seminary was getting "a facelift." They wanted to shift the seminary's emphasis, streamline its effectiveness, and increase its enrollment. Their strategy was to develop five core values which would keep the seminary focused, one of which was cultural relevance.

I wasn't surprised. These days it seems like every Christian organization wants to be culturally relevant. Why the shift? Church history tells a different story. Hundreds of years ago, groups of Christians, such as the monastics and ascetics, sought liberation from culture and attempted to escape it. They did not want to be relevant with culture. Evident even within the last one hundred years was one of the main tenets within fundamentalism—separation from culture.

Within many fundamentalist circles, cultural ignorance was seen as a badge of loyalty and purity of the faith, something to be displayed proudly.

But now we seem to have flipped the formula. We've exchanged the desire for cultural ignorance with the desire for cultural relevance — not necessarily a bad thing. There's nothing wrong with the desire for relevance. Christianity's primary purpose is by its very nature extremely relevant to the world. The problem comes when we're unable to define relevance. How can we achieve something if we're not sure what it means?

Consider the seminary dean's new core value: cultural relevance. By their very nature, core values are not supposed to be words on a wall but rather principles that shape what we do and how we interact with each other and strategies we employ to fulfill our mission. Core values are the practices we use (or should be using) every day in everything we do.

The dean, in his explanation, was extremely vague about what cultural relevance meant for him and his institution. This is all too common. Many organizations and churches have landed on cultural relevance as a value without dialoguing about the implications. For most, relevance is nothing more than the latest buzzword.

Do these institutions have a proposal to bring about relevance? Have they designated avenues that cultivate relevance? Have they thought through the ramifications of maintaining relevance once they've attained it? More important, do they have a way to quantify relevance in order to track it? Are there clear measurements that allow for evaluation with the hope of standardization?

Perhaps my questions sound a bit "businesslike," but I'm not apologizing. They're supposed to. When an organization (whether it be a church, parachurch, or seminary) develops core values, that organization has willingly entered into a business paradigm. Follow-up questions about plans, metrics, and definitions are the next logical step.

And even if relevance is difficult to define, we must achieve some clarity. If we do not, if we start out fuzzy on our definition of relevance, we'll be *that* much fuzzier on our destination.

Knowingly or unknowingly, when we fail to define relevance, we sidestep accountability. For how can we be accountable if we haven't defined relevance? Worse yet, without accountability and a means of measuring relevance, we often unrightfully assign ourselves the title of relevance. And since we haven't defined what it means in our situation, who can argue whether or not we've achieved it?

Relevance is a tricky thing.

We can't self-profess our way into it; we have to earn it. Relevance is something others believe about us, not what we believe about ourselves. It's kind of like humility. No one can accurately say they're humble. If they do, then they're not, even if they actually are. This is true for individuals, and it is true for churches as well. Putting "relevant" on a banner or business card is a trendy thing to do these days. But it's nothing more than a slogan until others grant us this attribute. A church can say it is relevant and even believe it's relevant. But unless the surrounding community believes this, that church isn't relevant.

Smoke and Mirrors

A dictionary at times offers more sense than the church. It defines relevance as "having significant and demonstrable bearing on facts or issues."[1] A relevant person is one who has a connection to or a bearing on the subject at hand.

Sounds like something positive. What Christ-follower wouldn't want to be relevant? Yet some Christians fear that *relevant* is just a synonym for *sin,* while others mistake trendy haircuts and worship

styles for real connection with hurting people. It seems clear that
Christians need to be — are commanded to be — relevant so long
as it is understood as having a significant, godly impact on the surrounding world.

But how? How do we impact the world positively without it impacting us negatively?

Countless words are spoken and written each year about how to
be relevant, and few of them are helpful. I once attended a pastor's
conference at which a speaker told us that our churches would be
relevant once we decorated with some hanging sheets and lit a few
candles. Oh, and he recommended a fog machine too. He confused
externals with internals, a confusion which, unfortunately, extends
back in time for millennia.

People in Jesus' day weren't all that different. They too wanted
to know the meaning of relevance. On one particular day, a lawyer
asked Jesus a question. A lawyer's main job was to interpret the Law.[2]
The lawyer's expertise gained him special privileges, like the right to
teach Hebrew youth and influence future generations.

The Jews had an increasing amount of Law they were respon-
sible to uphold. Most of us have heard of the Ten Commandments,
but first-century Jews recognized hundreds of other commandments
based primarily upon the Torah — the first five books of the Old
Testament, also known as the Pentateuch.

Interpreting these laws was no small task. Lawyers became in-
creasingly significant simply because so many laws existed. Although
most Jews were well-versed in the Torah, often there was a need for
someone to answer particular questions related to the Law. Two of
the prevailing questions of the day were: Which is the greatest com-
mandment? and What must one do to inherit eternal life?

During his time on earth, people asked Jesus both of these questions (see Matthew 22:35–36 and Luke 10:25). One day, trying to
test Jesus, a lawyer asked, "What must I do to inherit eternal life?"

Jesus put it back on the lawyer. He said, "What is written in the Law? How do you read it?"

It was a win-win situation. Jesus wanted to hear the lawyer's heart, and the lawyer wanted to hear himself talk. The lawyer took the opportunity to flaunt his expertise by giving the standard answer: "'Love the Lord your God with all your heart and with all your soul and with all your strength and with all your mind'; and, 'Love your neighbor as yourself.'"

He should have quit while he was ahead. Instead, in the presence of the famed Rabbi, he dared to ask a second question — this one probably with the wrong motive. "And who is my neighbor?" The Bible says he asked this question just to make himself look spiritual in everyone else's eyes (Luke 10:25 – 27, 29).

As an orthodox Jew, the lawyer probably expected Jesus to give the standard answer: "Your neighbor is your fellow Jew."[3] This wouldn't have been a wrong answer. The Law does say, "Do not seek revenge or bear a grudge against one of your people, but love your neighbor as yourself. I am the LORD" (Leviticus 19:18).

This law seems to say that you are to take care of your own. But that's not the only thing the Law says, and it's one more example of how Separatists and Conformists can run into trouble by reading only selected verses in the Bible. There are a variety of other passages where God reveals his heart concerning societal outsiders (Deuteronomy 1:16 – 17). God didn't allow the Israelites to show partiality for other Israelites within their judicial system or their economic system (Leviticus 19:33 – 35). God didn't distinguish between Jew and Gentile.[4] Rather, God summed up the way Jews should treat Gentiles: "The stranger who resides with you shall be to you as the native among you, and you shall love him as yourself" (Leviticus 19:34 NASB).

God's pattern is to take an active role in loving the marginalized, the outcast, and the poor. He reaches out to them before they reach out to him. The Jews should have known this. It was in the pages of Scripture along with all the other words they so meticulously memorized. But we can tell, by the lawyer's dialogue with Jesus, that the religious and cultural leaders seemed to have forgotten that part of Scripture.

So to answer the lawyer's second question, Jesus told a story:

> A man was going down from Jerusalem to Jericho, when he fell into the hands of robbers. They stripped him of his clothes, beat him and went away, leaving him half dead. A priest happened to be going down the same road, and when he saw the man, he passed by on the other side. So too, a Levite, when he came to the place and saw him, passed by on the other side. But a Samaritan, as he traveled, came where the man was; and when he saw him, he took pity on him. He went to him and bandaged his wounds, pouring on oil and wine. Then he put the man on his own donkey, took him to an inn and took care of him. The next day he took out two silver coins and gave them to the innkeeper. "Look after him," he said, "and when I return, I will reimburse you for any extra expense you may have."
>
> Luke 10:30−35

Jesus' story sent shock waves through his audience. If it seems tame to us, it's only because we aren't considering its implications. In this story, the traditional Jewish heroes, the Levite and the priest, are made out to be villains. And the traditional Jewish villain, the Samaritan, is made out to be a hero. Jesus' audience got the message, even if they didn't *get* the message. This is obvious from the lawyer's answer at the end of the story. Jesus asked him, "Which of these three do you think proved to be a neighbor to the man who fell into the robbers' hands?" The lawyer, probably unwilling to give any credit to a Samaritan by name — and admit to the corresponding changes required in his beliefs and actions — replied, "The one who showed mercy toward him" (Luke 10:36−37 NASB).

Jews had a right to despise the Samaritans—or so they thought. For starters, the Samaritans were descendants from the northern tribe of Israel who had ignored God's command and married foreigners, thus tainting their pure Jewish lineage. If that wasn't bad enough, the Samaritans had abandoned the Jewish nation in its greatest time of need—when the Jews were attempting to rebuild the walls of Jerusalem.

The Jews not only despised the Samaritans as a people but wanted nothing to do with their land as well. Most Jews avoided traveling through Samaria. Still, if an itinerary demanded a quick pass-through, before returning to their homeland, many Jews would shake their garments thoroughly to expel any Samaritan dust inadvertently collected during transit. No need to pollute the Promised Land or the promised people.

Despite all this drama going on in the background, the melody line of Jesus' story was undeniable.

If we could ask the unfortunate man in Jesus' story which of the other characters was most relevant to him, what would he say? He would say it was the one who stopped and got off the donkey, cleansed his wounds, attended to his needs, and paid his medical bills. He would say it was the Samaritan.

The temple-employed priest and the Scripture-spouting Levite were entirely irrelevant to the injured man. The Samaritan, the social outcast and "irrelevant" man of the day, became relevant when he displayed love for someone else.

The injured Jewish man was a liability to the Samaritan—infringing upon his time, task, and financial resources. Yet the Samaritan stopped everything in order to be inconvenienced by a Jew, someone who would, by tradition, hate him. He chose to get involved, and in so doing the Samaritan became relevant.

This is exactly what we're called to do.

Four and No More

Relevance has little to do with externals. It wasn't the Samaritan's clothes, vocabulary, nationality, or wealth that made him culturally relevant. The Samaritan and the Jew didn't even worship in the same way or in the same place (John 4:20). Yet all these barriers were broken as love was embodied in bandages, compassion, and coins.

To bring it into our context, relevance isn't about the brand of clothing we wear or the music we listen to. It's not about our vocabulary or even the exact shape of our theology. These are externals. Relevance is fundamentally *internal*. It's having the courage and the grace to look at a wounded man and stop to help. From that internal decision flows our relevant actions. As depicted in the story of the good Samaritan, what makes us relevant is our love for God and people.

Can it be that simple?

It can. But it turns out that it's anything but simple to put into practice. Loving people — *all* people — is one of the hardest things we can conceive of doing. And *loving* God — with all our heart, soul, and mind — well, that makes loving people look easy.

Humor me for a second. If you had to use four words to synthesize the entire Bible, what four words would you use? "A big rule book"? "Interesting stories about God"? If Jesus had only four words to use, he would have used "love God, love people" (see Matthew 22:37–40). Agreeing with Jesus, Paul wrote in one of his letters, "The entire law is summed up in a single command: 'Love your neighbor as yourself'" (Galatians 5:14).

"Love God, love people" might not sound sufficiently complicated, or interesting, or philosophical, but its depth is bottomless. And everything we do depends on it.

How can I be relevant to the teenage mom who rents a studio down the street? It won't be by downloading the latest song. What might make me relevant is for my wife and me to ask this young mom for her grocery list and go shopping for her. We could even pick up something else—the tab. It's our love for her and the God who made her that will bridge the cultural, socioeconomic, and religious barriers. Love is the language of relevance.

In his letter to the Corinthians, the apostle Paul demystifies the debate on what makes a person relevant. He informs us that we can have incredible spiritual gifts. We can sport a brilliant intellect, bestow endless faith. We can give away all our possessions or even sacrifice our very lives. Still, if we lack love, we're entirely empty (1 Corinthians 13:1–3).

It's not what we do, what we say, what we know, or what we give that makes us relevant. It's not about being trendy or current. There's a language that runs deeper than our music, movies, and media. It's the language of love, and unless we speak it fluently—with our lives, our actions, and our beliefs—our message will never be understood.

The Proverbial Donkey

Let me give an illustration about donkeys. In Jesus' story, the Good Samaritan was traveling somewhere. He had a task and a destination. His mode of transportation was a beast, a donkey. His donkey represented the ability to reach his intended goal. What matters is that he got off the animal. He put his task on hold and became relevant to someone in desperate need of some love.

It reminds me of my daily schedule. Just like you, I have places to go and people to see. We all have tasks and agendas, and the last thing we want is interruptions. I imagine the Samaritan was no different. And just like the Samaritan, we'll be relevant only when get off our proverbial ... um ... *donkeys* and love people.

Should we be surprised that love is the language of relevance?

Not if we consider Christ. It was his love for each person in the world that caused him to cross space, time, and culture. Like the Good Samaritan, he stooped down to heal hurt; he responded in love and, in so doing, became the most relevant person to ever live.

Aren't you glad Jesus not only told a story but also chose to enter your story and mine? On the road of life, our neighbor is lying wounded in need of our help.

How will we respond?

CHAPTER 5

THE SPIRITUAL ASPIRIN

Let's say I have a massive headache. If you were a compassionate person, what would you do for me? You'd probably hunt down some aspirin. That's what you do when someone has a headache, right?

Well, today it's most likely what you would do, but five hundred years ago you would have done something entirely different, depending on your culture. Perhaps you would have given me a cool rag to wrap around my head—less effective than aspirin, but not bad. But if you were from a certain place in Peru, you might use a process called *trepanation* and drill a hole in my skull. Thanks, but I'll take the aspirin instead!

Paradigms are that powerful. They provide us with a set of lenses so that we can make sense of something. In my headache scenario, a common paradigm helps us agree that a small pill will ease my pain if taken at the right time in the proper dosage. We might not understand the chemical reasons that make aspirin work, but we understand enough of the paradigm to benefit from it—namely that if we have a headache and take the painkiller, we'll feel better.

A paradigm is a mental framework built from what we commonly think, believe, and do. Paradigms are the way we understand everyday life, and we tend to share them with others. We have paradigms for all kinds of things: electricity, the economy, education, even eBay.

Sadly, the church often fails to build a paradigm concerning relevance. Within our whole dialogue regarding the sickness of irrelevance, at times it seems like our solutions have been more on par with drilling skulls than giving aspirin, and that's got to change.

And so we're going to build a paradigm that will help us understand how to live in the world but not be of it. Then over the next several chapters we'll compare and contrast an ineffective paradigm, which yields irrelevance, with an effective paradigm, which yields relevance.

Cultured Christians

Thinking of a teeter-totter or seesaw will help us as we build our paradigm, piece by piece. Let's start by looking at the relationship between Christianity and culture.

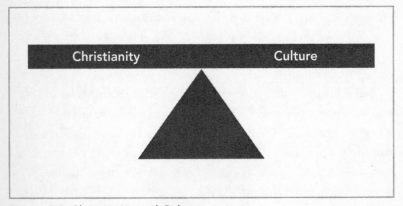

Figure 5.1: Christianity and Culture

Most people believe Christianity and culture are incompatible —like a bus full of Michigan and Ohio State football fans on game day in November. People assume Christianity and culture are in direct opposition with one another and that more of one equals less of the other. This thinking certainly simplifies things. Yet biblically, theologically, and historically it's inaccurate.

True, there is a distinction between Christianity and culture. The gospel of John makes it clear that Christ, the central person of Christianity, acknowledged his distinction from culture (John 17:14, 16). He said, "You are from below; I am from above. You are of this world; I am not of this world" (John 8:23).

Besides, if there were no distinction, there would be no need to convert to Christianity. Residents of culture would simply be Christians just because they're born. This thought obviously conflicts with Scripture, which continually calls us *from* something *to* something.

But just because culture is distinct from Christianity, that doesn't mean it's *absent* from Christianity. Culture is the collective attitudes, customs, and beliefs that distinguish one group of people from another. So Christianity necessarily includes culture. And culture isn't the enemy because, according to the Bible, our battle isn't against "flesh and blood" (Ephesians 6:12). Rather, culture is intended to be the venue in which we live out our Christianity.

The perceived opposition between Christianity and culture stems from a dualistic, Western worldview that divides life into categories—categories like *sacred* or *secular*. Within this view, prayer and evangelism are spiritual activities, while exercise and eating are secular. Christian schoolteachers and missionaries have spiritual vocations, while businesspeople and computer programmers have secular ones. God shows up in spiritual places, like church and nature; he is absent from secular venues, like sports arenas.

This type of worldview is toxic on multiple levels. The theologian Abraham Kuyper recognized these dangers and said, "There is not an inch in the entire domain of our human life of which Christ, who is sovereign of all, does not proclaim, 'Mine!'"[1] Kuyper understood that all of life is God's and that God shows up in every place, no matter what we assume about it.

As God's people, we're called to fight against this human tendency to compartmentalize, represented in what I call the Fragmented/Dualistic worldview. We must replace it with a worldview that harmonizes with God's Word—one that believes Christianity and culture should be integrated, what I call the Connected/Holistic worldview. This worldview doesn't allow a separation between the sacred and the secular; instead they're intimately related to one another.

The Connected/Holistic worldview was embodied by God's people, the Israelites, in the Old Testament. For example, a Hebrew farmer would recite a special prayer (Deuteronomy 26:5–10) in order to remind himself that the occupation of tilling the soil is sacred. The Connected/Holistic worldview is also consistent with God's people, the church, in the New Testament. In fact, the apostle Paul instructs local churches in this same vein, in light of his strong Hebrew upbringing. "So whether you eat or drink or whatever you do, do it all for the glory of God" (1 Corinthians 10:31). This generous worldview affects everything, from agriculture to education to technology. It includes the way we mow our lawns, the way we view our sexuality, and the way we treat our neighbors.

These two worldviews, the Fragmented/Dualistic and the Connected/Holistic, are completely different. One views Christianity as part of life, the other views Christianity as all of life. Notice the contrast below:

Worldview	Fragmented/Dualistic	Connected/Holistic
Relationship of Christianity/Culture	In opposition with one another	Integrated with one another
Mind-set	Greek/Western	Hebrew/Eastern

Worldview	Fragmented/Dualistic	Connected/Holistic
Motto	Some things are spiritual	All things are spiritual
Concept of belief and action	What I believe can be different from what I do.	What I believe is defined by what I do.
Concept of categories	For Christians there are two categories: Sacred/Secular.	For Christians there is only one category: Sacred.
Concept of priesthood	Professional ministers	Priesthood of all believers
Concept of prayer	Material is bad and immaterial is good. Our prayers sanctify the material.	All things, material and immaterial, can be good. Our prayers bless the God who grants us the material.

Figure 5.2: Worldview Comparison

Let's look a little deeper at what a few of these contrasts mean for us and for the church.

Concept of Belief and Action

Worldview affects every area of our lives, including the way we read the Bible. Certain books of the Bible—like James—pose a problem if read in light of the Fragmented/Dualistic worldview.

Throughout history, some Christians have had a problem with the book of James, believing that it dismisses salvation by grace through faith and exchanges it for a religion oriented in "works." The reformer Martin Luther even wanted the book of James to be cut out of the Bible! These people have read James through the lens of a Western mind-set. When read this way, James seems to say that people receive salvation by doing activities, like feeding the poor and caring for orphans and widows (James 1:27). The concept of "receiving salvation" is interesting all by itself—as if we get it and can check it off our to-do list, as if once saved we just kill time on earth, as if it's all about the next life and not this one too.

We'll get to this whole concept later on in our dialogue. For now, let's see what the book of James seems to say if studied from an Eastern mind-set, the framework in which it was written. For starters, it dispels the type of erroneous thinking that fails to recognize the truth—namely, that faith and works are two sides of the same coin. The author James doesn't allow us the luxury of a dualism between belief and action, theory and reality. Rather, James links the two. What we do reveals what we believe, and what we believe is revealed by what we do. We're not saved by works, but our works prove that we're saved.

The authors of *The Ascent of a Leader* demonstrate the distinction between these two mind-sets:

> In Hebrew philosophy, a belief was not a belief until it was acted on. In Greek philosophy, belief could be separated from action. Thought and action suffered a painful divorce into upper and lower stories of existence. Greek thinking led to dualism, a separation between the material and spiritual aspects of life. Hebrew philosophy seems comparatively simple. No dualism. No separation. If you love someone, you will meet her need. If you meet someone's need, you love her. Hebrews did not separate the heart from the mind, or belief from action. They were one in the same.[2]

The Connected/Holistic worldview celebrates the marriage between knowing and doing. As a result it invites proponents to live rich, integrated lives. The Fragmented/Dualistic worldview divorces what we know from what we do, producing lives that are shallow and hypocritical.

Concept of Categories

Let's shoot straight. Categories confuse both the world *and* the church. If everything is spiritual, then categories are just an attempt to prevent God from showing up. As if we could stop him even if we wanted to! Everything is a spiritual decision, including how I handle my finances and (even though it sounds odd) how I handle my dog (Proverbs 12:10).

The scholar Erasmus understood this type of interconnectivity and explained its implications. "Socrates brought philosophy down from heaven to earth; I have brought it even into the games, informal conversations, and drinking parties."[3] From his perspective, God—and the study of God—should be, and in fact was, involved in every aspect of culture, even in leisure and the arts.

Unfortunately, for Christians, integrating theology with the arts hasn't always been the pattern, especially recently. Rather, many churches seem to have kicked artists out. Sometimes it's blatant, but more often it's subtle. We tend to place an emphasis upon certain gifts, like preaching, teaching, or leading worship. We downplay—or even exclude—other gifts like visual art, dance, and literature.

We forget that God emphasized the arts. He didn't lack creativity regarding his own handiwork. And he equipped certain artists in a special way. He didn't spare many details when designing the Tent of Meeting or the ark of the testimony (Exodus 31:1–11). Moses then told the Israelites:

> The LORD has chosen Bezalel son of Uri, the son of Hur, of the tribe of Judah, and he has filled him with the Spirit of God, with skill, ability and knowledge in all kinds of crafts—to make artistic designs for work in gold, silver and bronze, to cut and set stones, to work in wood and to engage in all kinds of artistic craftsmanship. And he has given both him and Oholiab son of Ahisamach, of the tribe of Dan, the ability to teach others.

He has filled them with skill to do all kinds of work as craftsmen, designers, embroiderers in blue, purple and scarlet yarn
and fine linen, and weavers — all of them master craftsmen and
designers.

Exodus 35:30–35

If God is so creative, why are we so ... uncreative?

In recent times, followers of Christ haven't been known for leading the way in the exploration of the arts. But this is only a symptom,
not the problem. Over time the church has devolved into a place of
artistic bankruptcy. And when we fail to take the arts seriously, we
export an impoverished theology.

Artists inherently know this. For many of them, the church is the
last place they would go in order to feel encouraged and supported in
their craft. The arts get placed on the back burner because they don't
seem practical or, sadly, because they're too risky.

Maybe part of the problem is that, as the church, we don't know
how to benefit from the arts. Maybe we've gotten away without the
arts for so long we've forgotten what incorporating them would even
look like.

I know for me this whole conversation seemed a bit fuzzy until
I took some risks within my local context. I used to be the youth
pastor at my church, and leading a midweek youth service was part
of my job. I knew the teens desperately needed a venue to connect
with each other and with God, and one more lecture from me wasn't
going to cut it.

I spent some time in prayer and came to the conclusion that I
should try to incorporate the arts. So the next Wednesday evening
I dimmed the lights, put on some soft music, and passed out crayons
and markers. I asked the teens to spend some time drawing their
relationship with God.

Then I held my breath and waited.

I thought they wouldn't take it seriously and expected a crayon fight to break out at any moment.

Only it didn't.

Instead, there was a solid twenty minutes of silence. Guys and girls spread out throughout the room in order to create their masterpieces. When the allotted time expired, I invited the teens to stand up and share their pictures with the rest of the group.

Again I held my breath and waited; no one budged.

A high school junior named Chris finally broke the silence. I couldn't help but groan. Chris was one of those kids who always goofed off, hardly my ideal choice to lead in this experimental sharing time.

Chris stood up with his head hanging, looking somewhat defeated. He had drawn, with professional-like accuracy, a picture of Santa Claus, rosy cheeks and all. I frowned, convinced he hadn't taken my challenge seriously.

Ten seconds later I ate my words.

Chris went on to explain that he chose Santa Claus to reflect his relationship with God because lately he had been coming to God only when he needed a hookup. For Chris, his relationship with God had evolved into one big transactional experience.

The teens sat stunned, mouths hanging open, touched by the authenticity of their peer's confession. After he sat down, a student named Sarah stood up. She showed us her picture and in tears explained her motivation. Filling the entire page was a beautifully drawn eye with lashes and one teardrop in the corner. A closer look revealed that the pupil of the eye, drawn with intentional subtly, reflected one solitary cross on a menacing hill. Evidently, Sarah's picture reflected her own indebtedness to Jesus for his sacrifice on her behalf.

Later that year we took a couple more risks within our teen service. One evening I read a verse out of Corinthians ("When you [come together], each one has a psalm, has a teaching ..." [1 Corinthians 14:26 NASB]). Then we provided some time and space for the teens to write their own psalm to God. After fifteen or twenty minutes they read their psalms aloud. Through this venue the teens again connected with God and with each other. I'm banking on the fact that our expressions of art were a pleasing aroma to God.

We must not forget that the arts are God's gift to us. Beginning in the Old Testament, God purposed their use within the context of corporate worship. The arts are tools meant to tap into the way we think and feel about God. Shame on us if we're too afraid to infuse the arts into our churches.

The Connected/Holistic worldview celebrates all of life, including the arts, as a potential means of glorifying God. Proponents are invited to explore, create, and incorporate all of who they are into their relationship with God.

Concept of Priesthood

The church once honored believers who had vocations "outside" the church, not labeling them as second-class citizens just because they weren't pastors or missionaries. Throughout history, whenever the church embraced the Connected/Holistic worldview, we made great strides in impacting the world. During the Reformation, for example, Martin Luther understood the potential for new believers to transform their world for Christ. One day a shoemaker came to Luther wondering if he should quit his job and take on a more "spiritual profession" since he was now a follower of Christ—a question people in all kinds of professions ask today. Luther said, "Make a good shoe and sell it at a fair price, in this God is glorified."[4]

Luther cut through layers of fuzzy thinking with that one comment. He recognized that spirituality is not limited to a specific job or location. Instead, spirituality is with us wherever we go, because spirituality should be who we *are*.

Times have changed. Today we make frequent distinctions between professional ministers, called clergy, and everyone else. This clergy/laity paradigm only exists within the Fragmented/Dualistic worldview. In this worldview, evangelists, bishops, and chaplains are considered more spiritual simply because of their profession. This causes serious harm to the church. While the paid professionals run the church, everyone else is invited to sit on the bench and spectate. Laity only consumes and critiques. Should we be surprised, when things aren't exactly according to their liking, they simply pack up and move to the church down the street?

Rising leaders are forced to choose between "sacred" and "secular" jobs. Those who choose sacred jobs receive accolades; those who choose secular occupations receive guilt. College students choosing career paths which lead them into "full-time" vocational ministry receive more from the church: more prayer, more attention, more scholarships. The next generation of believers sits in the congregation, not knowing what career path they should choose, wondering how to be a good Christian if they don't want to be professional ministers.

The Bible doesn't support the clergy/laity paradigm. Instead, it refers to all believers—male/female, young/old, rich/poor, black/white—as priests (Galatians 3:28; 1 Peter 2:5, 9). All are empowered as ministers within whatever sphere they find themselves. And because God fills the entire earth, every vocation has the potential to honor, glorify, and discover him (Jeremiah 23:24).[5]

When followers of Jesus accurately see themselves as priests, everyone wins. The church wins because believers are empowered to use their spiritual gifts. The body of Christ functions as just that—a body, rather than a single body part. Pastors are no longer the experts who have co-opted the priesthood. Rather, they fulfill their primary job—to equip other believers for the work of the ministry (Ephesians 4:11–13). And the world wins too. Millions of Christ-followers are unleashed to bestow compassion and kindness upon their neighbors. Believers can no longer use the excuse of "That's not *my* job." Instead, they're liberated and mobilized to fulfill the Great Commission which Christ gave to all people, not just to pastors.

Concept of Prayer

Our worldview also affects the way we pray. The Fragmented/ Dualistic worldview sees the immaterial as good and the material as bad. Because the material is bad, it must be sanctified. People are expected to pray in order to bless food, drink, and other material things. An example prayer before a meal might sound something like: "Lord, we ask you to bless this food to our bodies."

The Connected/Holistic worldview doesn't see the need to bless material things in order to sanctify them. Everything is already blessed. According to Marvin R. Wilson, a leading scholar in Christian-Jewish relations at Gordon College, Hebrew prayers centered on someone rather than something. Hebrew prayers "focused only on blessing God, the Creator and Giver. The Gospels indicate that Jesus followed this same custom."[6] The Gospel writer Mark used the Greek word *eulogeo* when recording that Jesus bestowed a blessing on God when he broke the five loaves and two fishes. According to this worldview, an example prayer before a meal might sound something like: "Lord, we bless you for this food you've given to us."

A Relevant Paradigm

In the last chapter we defined relevance as loving God and people. In this chapter we'll add to our picture by illustrating relevance. Notice the paradigm below.

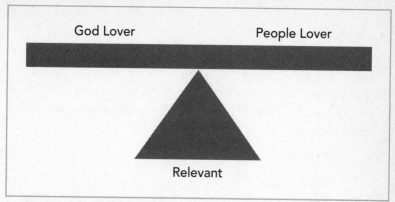

Figure 5.3: Biblical Relevance

In the paradigm, there's no way to determine where loving God begins and where loving people stops. This is intentional. The Bible says we can't have one without the other. We can't love God and not love our neighbor.

> If someone says, "I love God," and hates his brother, he is a liar; for the one who does not love his brother whom he has seen, cannot love God whom he has not seen.
>
> 1 John 4:20 NASB

Neither can we fully love our neighbor without loving God.

> Beloved, let us love one another, for love is from God; and everyone who loves is born of God and knows God. The one who does not love does not know God, for God is love.
>
> 1 John 4:7–8 NASB

Just as Christianity and culture are interrelated, so are loving God and loving people. Although loving God and loving people are distinct from one another, they're not in opposition to one another.

We've been slowly building the paradigm one piece at a time. It took a while to get here, but now we can finally put together the elements of this model.

We first needed to understand the biblical definition of relevance: loving God and loving people. Next, we needed to discover the importance of integrating our Christianity with our culture. And now we're ready to discover the complete fine line paradigm: how to live in the world but not be of it.

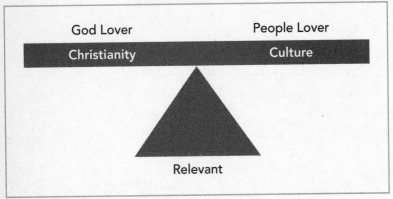

Figure 5.4: The Fine Line Paradigm

The power of a paradigm surfaces when we use it, so let's try on the fine line paradigm and walk around a bit. We'll look at two critical components related to our paradigm: The Fulcrum and The Balancing Act.

The Fulcrum

Remember middle school science class? The fulcrum is the point, or support, on which the board of our teeter-totter pivots and balances. It prevents the teeter-totter from remaining in a fixed position. In the fine line paradigm, this pivotal point is the life of a real person, the place where the theoretical confronts the practical.

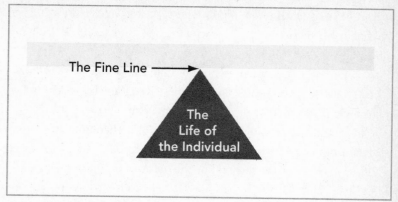

Figure 5.5: The Fulcrum

Up until this point, our dialogue about paradigms has been a bit philosophical. And as long as it remains that way, it's powerless. But when a person joins the equation, the fulcrum, that pivotal point of balance in a person's life, takes on new meaning. The fulcrum is that moment of truth, the fine line. More than any other part of the paradigm, our relation to the fine line reveals our level of relevance. When we live as God lovers and people lovers, and when we integrate our Christianity with our culture, then we, as relevant Christians, live out our paradigm before the watching world.

The Balancing Act

Yet our tendency is to quickly become unbalanced. As you know, the ends of a teeter-totter move up and down when people or objects are placed on them. In a symbolic sense this happens with our paradigm as well. We're constantly bouncing toward one side or the other. Yet rather than attempting to regain balance, our tendency is to fall to one side and remain motionless, resting in that unbalanced extreme. When life hits, we lean toward being a God lover *or* a people lover. Our loyalty leans toward our Christianity *or* our culture. We exchange the *and* for the *or*—and in that moment we become irrelevant.

So how do we stay balanced?

Bad news. On our own, it's impossible. As humans we're hardwired to always lean toward an extreme, toward the life of a Separatist or a Conformist. It's our default mechanism.

But balance is possible. It's *maintained* not through a plan or a program but only through a person. Paul explains this in a letter read by believers everywhere, "For the grace of God that brings salvation has appeared to all [people]. It teaches us to say 'No' to ungodliness and worldly passions, and to live self-controlled, upright and godly lives in this present age" (Titus 2:11–12). When we take a microscope to this passage, it becomes clear that "the grace of God that brings salvation" is the incarnation of Jesus. Jesus Christ is the literal manifestation of God's grace.

Only Jesus, not a list of rules, can bring balance to our lives. Jesus teaches us how to say "no" to certain things like ungodliness and worldly lusts. Jesus teaches us how to say "yes" to other things like living self-controlled, upright, and godly lives in the present age.

The word *self-controlled* is important to our dialogue. I'm more familiar with this word than I ever wanted to be, thanks to one of my former professors, Dr. Bateman. Several years ago in Greek class I was assigned a word study on "self-controlled." Initially I wasn't too thrilled about spending eight hours researching the obscure Greek word *sophronos* and its usage throughout historical literature.

God had something else in mind. He used that word to reveal the fear and control I exhibited in my walk of "faith." At that time in my life, I was trusting in my personal rules for every aspect of my life—including the movies I watched, the books I read, the people I hung out with, and the music I listened to. What I didn't realize was that in my pursuit of God and personal holiness, I'd become irrelevant to people and the world around me. I prided myself in attaining a pure faith but was blinded to sin that popped up in so many other areas of my life. I didn't know it, but I was a Separatist.

Then along came *sophronos*—self-controlled, temperate, or moderate. Oftentimes it's translated as sober.

What characterizes someone who's not sober? Unbalance. I'll admit to occasionally watching *COPS* on television. When the police officer pulls over the guy for a suspected DUI, she has him walk the line. If he can walk that fine line, proving he's sober, then he's not a threat to himself or those around him. But if he can't, if he's out of balance, then watch out. He's immediately removed in handcuffs.

When we're unbalanced, we're not only irrelevant but we're a threat to ourselves and those around us. The world is filled with people who have been wounded by out-of-balance Separatists and Conformists. I have been, and I'll bet you have too. Sadly, I've been the one doing the wounding at times. We need to stop pretending that this doesn't happen. It does—often—and it discredits both Christ and his church.

Now that we know the Greek word *sophronos*, let's look at that verse in Titus again. The apostle Paul writes in Titus 2:11–12 that Christ teaches us how to live a balanced life. He said that the grace of God has appeared (in the person of Jesus Christ) *and* teaches us to live self-controlled (balanced) lives in the present age.

As we consider Christ, it's evident that he was a balanced person. Walking the earth, he walked the fine line. In solitude he fellowshipped with the Father, and in community he hung out with the crowd (John 5:19–27; Mark 6:33–44). He had meals with Mary and Martha and debates with the teachers of the Law (John 12:1–2; Mark 11:27–33). He raised the dead and at times retreated from those who needed healing (John 11:43–44; Mark 6:31).

Jesus not only modeled a balanced life but he also expected it from his followers. He exhorted them, "I am sending you out like sheep among wolves. Therefore be as shrewd as snakes and as innocent as doves" (Matthew 10:16).

Still, we're never going to master balance. We'll never arrive at some place where we love God and people perfectly, and we'll never flawlessly integrate our Christianity with our culture.

We're not supposed to. God doesn't want us to. He wants us to struggle, because it's within the struggle that we learn dependence. Our irrelevant extremes force us back to Jesus, the balanced one.

The relevant one.

Get Ready for Camp

We've still got a long way to go. If we're going to transform the world around us, we need to first experience some transformation. We need to discover why we are where we are. We need to look in the mirror and understand the extremes that rob us of our relevance.

Within the next two chapters we'll do just that. We'll look at the irrelevance and unbalance that characterize the Separatist and the Conformist camps. The illustrations and descriptions are intentionally extreme. My guess is that you're not *that* irrelevant. Neither am I. But if we're honest, we'll see a little bit of ourselves in one, or both, of these camps.

CHAPTER 6

FIFTY-FOOT COLUMN

People do the strangest things to make a name for themselves.

In May 2002, illusionist David Blaine stood on top of a stone column in New York's Bryant Park for thirty-four hours and twenty-three minutes.[1] But Blaine might not be the creative genius that you think. He borrowed the idea of standing on a column from a guy who's been dead for over fifteen hundred years. And better yet, this guy didn't stay on his column for hours or even days. Simeon Stylites stayed on his for over thirty-six years![2]

While Blaine may have been motivated by fame, Stylites was motivated by something a little less common. As an ascetic, he wanted to escape the evil of the world. He didn't have success living horizontally in his culture, so he attempted to escape evil by living vertically with God. He knew no other way to achieve spiritual success than to literally remove himself from the world by sitting on top of a stone column.

It didn't work. In fact, pilgrims and tourists — the very culture he'd been trying to escape — clustered around his pillar. Stylites didn't seem to mind the attention, as he addressed the crowd twice a day. His disciples wanted to be near him so much they placed a ladder alongside the column. So much for escaping the world!

Welcome to (the) Camp

Separatists have been around for quite some time. Eve was the first and Stylites was probably the most creative. In Jesus' day, the Separatist camp was pervasive—they were a group of religious leaders called Pharisees. They created elaborate laws. But rather than being impressed, Jesus was appalled. He let them know: "They tie up heavy, cumbersome loads and put them on other people's shoulders, but they themselves are not willing to lift a finger to move them" (Matthew 23:4 TNIV).

The Pharisees didn't start out all that bad. Separatists rarely do. They had an intense passion for the Law, for personal holiness, and for following God. But their knowledge of the Law soon prevented them from getting to know God. As odd as it sounds, their pursuit of purity splintered their relationship with God. It's as if they started to rely on *what* they knew and forgot *who* they were supposed to know. They replaced God with religion. Their heads grew bigger while their hearts grew colder.

Things got so bad that when Jesus showed up, they didn't recognize him. These experts in the Law, the ones who knew all sorts of details about the coming Messiah, missed the Messiah even when he was standing right in front of them! This disconnection angered Jesus:

> You search the Scriptures because you think that in them you have eternal life; it is these that testify about Me; and you are unwilling to come to Me so that you may have life.
>
> John 5:39–40 NASB

Separatists try to prevent sin by adding to God's Word. The Pharisees much preferred God's Ten Commandments to the simpler summary—love God and love people. Eventually, however, even the specificity of the Ten Commandments wasn't enough, and so they began to construct what would become a total of 613 commandments, or mitzvoth,[3] well over half of which were negative thou-shalt-nots. Talk about raising the bar!

Stylites measured up in this area as well. Literally. He changed the height of his column a number of times. The world just felt too close. His first column, with a small platform on top, started out about ten feet tall. He soon increased it to fifteen feet, then twenty, then thirty-six, and finally about fifty feet tall.[4]

This smells a lot like another story—the Tower of Babel. It's one more example of humanity trying to make it to God by our own effort. Whether with brick and mortar or rules and religion, our human efforts can't bring us closer to God.

There's nothing wrong with personal convictions. I have many of them. I stay away from certain things, even though the Bible doesn't command me to do so, simply because I don't want to go down a certain path that could lead to my downfall. Personal convictions aren't a problem in and of themselves. It matters how we *use* them. If I elevate my personal convictions to the same level as God's Word, then I'm in trouble. Pride always follows when our personal convictions supersede God's Word. We quickly become the hero in our own story, just like the Pharisees. And, like them, we no longer think we need God.

Personal convictions are just that: personal. It's the Holy Spirit's job—not mine—to lead, guide, and convict each believer.

An example of how convictions can play out in our lives is in the use of alcohol. Although we should exercise wisdom and respon-sibility (bodily, emotionally, spiritually, legally, and socially) when considering whether to consume alcohol, we should also recognize that the Bible never prohibits its use. The Bible actually permits it, forbidding only drunkenness (Ephesians 5:18). It's fine for people to have a personal conviction to abstain from alcohol. The problem comes when their conviction is then imposed on others. These people are adding to God's Word.

Some Separatists take this further and say that one should never go into a bar or restaurant that serves alcohol. A few Separatists even ban others from associating with people who drink alcohol—a rule that would have caused problems for Jesus.

These rules created by the Separatists end up preventing a person from achieving Christ's vision for the church—to reach people by loving people. Sadly, Separatists live up to their name—they remain separated from the world. They fail to impact their world because, like Simon Stylites, they attempt to leave it.

The apostle Paul knew it was impossible for believers to remove themselves from the world. But even if it were possible, he didn't want it to happen. The only group he wanted us to separate from was immoral people who profess they're Christ-followers.

> I wrote to you in my letter not to associate with sexually im-moral people—not at all meaning the people of this world who are immoral, or the greedy and swindlers, or idolaters. In that case you would have to leave this world. But now I am writing to you that you must not associate with any who claim to be fel-low believers but are sexually immoral or greedy, idolaters or slanderers, drunkards or swindlers. With such persons do not even eat.
>
> 1 Corinthians 5:9–11 TNIV

This passage seems confusing at first because we all sin. Is Paul telling us that we need to separate from everyone, even ourselves? Simeon Stylites thought so.

So that we don't misapply the Scriptures, let's look at the context. In 1 Corinthians 5, Paul wanted the Christians at Corinth to separate from a guy who was arrogant about sleeping with his stepmother. The purpose of separating from him was to demonstrate the severity of his sin. Love for him, not hate, fueled this separation.

Of course, we're all sinners and none of us is perfect. The difference is that when we become callous and arrogant about our sin, we can reach a point in our pride when God gives us "over in the sinful desires of [our] hearts" and eventually "to a depraved mind" (Romans 1:24, 28). At this point we become desensitized to our own wickedness. We think we're healthy when instead we're spiritually sick.

When this takes place, our community of faith has the opportunity to humbly and lovingly confront us with the hope that we'll turn from our sin. Paul writes,

> If anyone is caught in any trespass, you who are spiritual, restore such a one in a spirit of gentleness; *each one* looking to yourself, so that you too will not be tempted.
>
> Galatians 6:1 NASB

Throughout this whole confrontation process, the keywords are *lovingly* and *humbly*. If the person caught in the sin is unwilling to admit the sin and arrogantly ignores the attempts for confrontation in order to turn from the sin, then Jesus tells us to treat the individual "as you would a pagan or a tax collector" (Matthew 18:17).

But if the person does acknowledge the sin, which was the case for this man sleeping with his stepmother, then we must immediately "forgive and comfort him, so that he will not be overwhelmed by excessive sorrow" and "reaffirm [our] love for him" (2 Corinthians 2:7–8).

Jesus had this whole *lovingly* and *humbly* thing down cold. He pursued lost people — it's why he came, "to seek and to save what was lost" (Luke 19:10). It's why he told the Pharisees, "It is not those who are healthy who need a physician, but those who are sick; I did not come to call the righteous, but sinners" (Mark 2:17 NASB).

This is our call as well.

Jesus' love for the lost defined his ministry. It's why, when he began his public ministry, he chose to proclaim what editor and author Jim Wallis calls Jesus' "Nazareth manifesto"[5]:

The Spirit of the Lord is on me,
>   because he has anointed me
>   to preach good news to the poor.
He has sent me to proclaim freedom for the prisoners
>   and recovery of sight for the blind,
to release the oppressed,
>   to proclaim the year of the Lord's favor.

Luke 4:18–19

His Separatist listeners tried to shut him up:

All the people in the synagogue were furious when they heard this. They got up, drove him out of the town, and took him to the brow of the hill on which the town was built, in order to throw him down the cliff.

Luke 4:28–29

They were convicted when confronted with their own failures to fulfill God's call. But rather then acknowledging their sin and allowing God to transform them, they sought to kill him.

Deceived God Lovers

We used the fine line paradigm in the last chapter when looking at what it means to live a life of relevance. But all teeter-totters prefer unbalance. In the life of a Separatist, this produces irrelevance. Notice the pattern on page 73.

Separatists vary in degree. Some of us are only slightly irrelevant, struggling here and there. Others are full-blown, card-carrying Separatists. But all of us are unbalanced.

Where do we get the fuel for our fire? Interestingly enough, from the Bible. We take verses out of context while failing to balance them with the whole of Scripture. We approach the Bible with a preconceived grid that allows us to see only what we want to see.[6] We

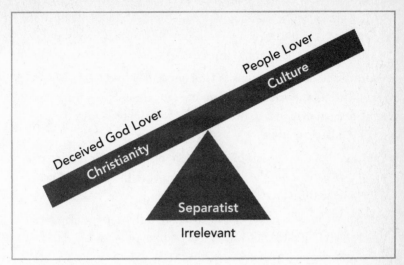

Figure 6.1: The Separatists

cling to certain verses as proof that God wants us to retreat from culture.

Below is some of our often used ammo:

You adulterous people, don't you know that friendship with the
world is hatred toward God? Anyone who chooses to be a
friend of the world becomes an enemy of God. (James 4:4)

Religion that God our Father accepts as pure and faultless is
this: to look after orphans and widows in their distress and to
keep oneself from being polluted by the world. (James 1:27)

Dear friends, I urge you, as aliens and strangers in the world,
to abstain from sinful desires, which war against your soul.
(1 Peter 2:11)

I have given them your word and the world has hated them, for
they are not of the world any more than I am of the world.
My prayer is not that you take them out of the world but
that you protect them from the evil one. They are not of the

world, even as I am not of it. Sanctify them by the truth; your word is truth. As you sent me into the world, I have sent them into the world. (John 17:14–18)

Grace and peace to you from God our Father and the Lord Jesus Christ, who gave himself for our sins to rescue us from the present evil age, according to the will of our God and Father. (Galatians 1:3–4)

The god of this age has blinded the minds of unbelievers, so that they cannot see the light of the gospel of the glory of Christ, who is the image of God. (2 Corinthians 4:4)

If anyone does not obey our instruction in this letter, take special note of him. Do not associate with him, in order that he may feel ashamed. (2 Thessalonians 3:14)

Do not love the world or anything in the world. If anyone loves the world, the love of the Father is not in him. For everything in the world—the cravings of sinful man, the lust of his eyes and the boasting of what he has and does—comes not from the Father but from the world. The world and its desires pass away, but the man who does the will of God lives forever. (1 John 2:15–17)

Our selective Scripture reading makes us drift toward an extreme and set up shop in the Separatist camp. Unbalance and irrelevance soon define our lives.

Characteristics

Those of us who lean toward the Separatist camp are guilty of certain characteristics. Three of our most common flaws are allowing rules to replace relationships, microscopes to replace mirrors, and performance to replace passion.

Rules give us the illusion of control. They allow us to hide our

hearts safely behind our lists of dos and don'ts. When we embrace rit-
ualistic rules, we inevitably forfeit a vibrant relationship with God.

Microscopes magnify the image of small objects. When used to
examine cells in the science lab, this is a good thing. But microscopes
shouldn't be used to examine everything. Jesus warned, "Why do you
look at the speck of sawdust in your brother's eye and pay no attention to the plank in your own eye?" (Matthew 7:3). Rather, we must
look in the mirror and deal with our own irrelevance first before we
comment on someone else's.

When we replace an inner passion for God with an outward performance for people, something is deeply wrong. We must stop act-
ing for one another and instead own up to our need for Jesus.

Out of This World

As Separatists, most of us sincerely want to be in the world but not
of the world. We want Jesus to be integrated into every facet of our
lives. We want to obey the Scriptures and not be "conformed to this
world" (Romans 12:2 NASB). These are all good desires. The problem is that we're just not sure how to do it. We experiment with a
variety of strategies in order to accomplish these desires, but most
of the time we fall far short.

One of our most extreme strategies, what I call the boycotting
strategy, occurs because of our fear of being tainted by the world.
This fear inspires us to simply withdraw from society. We get it in
our heads that God has called us to lives of suffering and persecution
for our radical stance against culture. And so it becomes our personal
cause to boycott every other cause. Unfortunately, we're defined only
for what we're against and not what we're for. Local churches end up
becoming the safe havens that enable us to get away from heathen
reprobates. Because we're consumed with fear, we set up fortresses
that permit us to escape reality and society.

A slightly more subtle strategy is that we try to sanctify even the most basic of activities, like drinking coffee, exercising, reading, shopping, or cleaning. Because we're uncomfortable with gray, we determine that everything must either be good or bad, black or white. After all, black or white categories allow us to attain our most coveted characteristic—control.

Gray is just too slippery—too dangerous. Gray poses a subtle attack that threatens to erode our personal purity. It must be eradicated. So when a gray activity arises, we create a Christian alternative that is somehow "sanctified." We buy the lie that gray activities become spiritual when they're Christianized, which is why I call this the Christianizing strategy.

But ironically, activities don't need to be sanctified. God created the world and he said it was good. Still, for some reason we feel compelled to Christianize every activity. We're no longer just content with coffee—now we have Christian coffee. We even have Christian vitamin companies and Christian workout clubs.

All this Christianizing is a bit odd. The Bible explains that our bodies are the temple of the Holy Spirit (1 Corinthians 6:19–20). And the apostle Paul acknowledged some benefit of physical exercise (1 Timothy 4:8). So taking care of our bodies, via vitamins or exercising, is already biblical—why do we need to resort to Christianizing?

As we peel back the layers behind our strategy of Christianizing, we begin to see that the dangers far outweigh the benefits. By causally dragging the name of Jesus into our hobbies, we confuse the watching world. It thinks of us as people just using God to make a buck. The Christian market is a multibillion-dollar pie, and the world wants a piece. *Newsweek*'s chief religion writer explains:

> I'll tell you what sells. It's been true for at least twenty-five
> years. Religion covers are always the first, second, and third

best-selling covers on the newsstand for *Time* and *Newsweek*. It's mostly Jesus who sells. For a while the pope sold, but the pope's too old and doesn't sell now. 'God and the Brain' sold, but mostly it's Jesus.[7]

This leads to the final strategy that we as Separatists ineffectively use in an attempt to try to live in the world but not be of the world. I call it the categorizing strategy. In order to not be conformed to the world, we categorize all art, music, philosophy, and entertainment as sacred or secular. We reject the secular categories and embrace the sacred ones.

This strategy is not only damaging, it's bad theology. While there is a world system set against the purposes and principles of God, not everything the world produces is bad. And the world, unlike portrayals in the movies, isn't made up of people who are all good or all bad. Writer Dan Buck has plenty to say about the dangers of creating categories. In his article "Getting Out of the Faith Ghetto," he writes:

> The problem is categories. We have categorized ourselves out of the world. Life is one category. Good music, good art, good health, and good prescription drugs are innately spiritual if they are in fact good. We don't need to label something Christian to the exclusion of the rest of the world for it to be good and pure. Because all things that are good and pure are of God. All truth is God's truth. If we are seeking God out of everything we do He will inevitably show up. He doesn't need labels or categories to find us and we shouldn't need them to find Him. Sure there are experiences that we should stay away from, but He has given us a mind, the Holy Spirit, and a body of believers to help us decipher what is of Him and what is not. Our categories have become the lazy Christian's guide to prudence. Truth. It is not supposed to be easy. Every experience, every person you meet, and every choice you make is part of the walk.[8]

Spirituality happens when we sit in our houses to watch a movie or read a book, not just when we sit in our churches to listen to a sermon. And God doesn't disappear when we digest literature, art, and music that is "secular." He's bigger than the categories we make.

We would do well to exercise caution. We need to be aware of things that might destroy us or things that aren't lovely, beautiful, or noble (1 Corinthians 6:12; Philippians 4:8 – 9). But just because something isn't patently Christian doesn't mean we should avoid it. God may intend for "worldly" things to play a role in our holiness. It's through wrestling over issues with him that we become stronger and sharper. That's what life is about: exercising faith and being in a dynamic relationship — not in a static religion.

I'm always a bit surprised when I see this reality come to life in the Scriptures. Two godly leaders, Moses and Daniel, grew up in fairly "secular" cultures. Egypt and Babylon weren't known as the most theologically orthodox hot spots of the day. Nonetheless, it was God who gave them success within their cultural education. Keep in mind, not only were Moses and Daniel exposed to "unchristian" art, education, and music, with God's backing they thrived within it.

> When he was placed outside, Pharaoh's daughter took him and brought him up as her own son. Moses was educated in all the wisdom of the Egyptians and was powerful in speech and action.
>
> Acts 7:21 – 22

> To these four young men God gave knowledge and understanding of all kinds of literature and learning. And Daniel could understand visions and dreams of all kinds.... In every matter of wisdom and understanding about which the king questioned them, he found them ten times better than all the magicians and enchanters in his whole kingdom.
>
> Daniel 1:17, 20

Of course in both of these examples there came a time for each man to draw a line in the sand and implement a cultural break. In Daniel's situation, he didn't defile himself with food from the king's table nor did he obey the king's edict which demanded that he refrain from praying to God. And in Moses' case, he eventually left it all: wealth, power, and his privileged position in Egypt. Still we can't ignore that both men received a rich cultural education within two incredibly idolatrous societies.

Categories may actually prevent holiness from showing up because, with categories, faith is no longer necessary. And no one can argue that Moses and Daniel were men whose lives were characterized by faith.

Jesus Java

What would Jesus think of all our Separatist strategies? If he were here in the flesh today, he'd probably contemplate the current situation while driving in a car purchased from the Christian car dealership with the latest Christian bumper sticker on the back. In his cup holder would sit a state-of-the-art Jesus Java mug that he picked up from the Christian coffeehouse. He would be decked out with the latest Christian T-shirt featuring a "creative" knockoff of a worldly slogan. He could journal all his thoughts in his Christian notebook with his Christian pencil that reads, "I'm a member of the J Team." If he was still confused, he could clear his mind with some Christian music on his MP3 player while on his way to the Christian bookstore. If things got overwhelming, he could get rid of some stress by using the treadmill at the Christian fitness club. But eventually, he'd get exhausted and need some Christian vitamins to help him reenergize and some Christian mints to freshen his breath. Later, he could watch Christian television while he grabbed the Christian phone book and ordered out for a pizza delivered by a Christian teenager who also drives a car with the latest Christian bumper sticker that reads "Jesus is my co-pilot."

Perhaps only a smidge extreme, the above scenario smells strangely familiar. So what does Jesus think of our Christian subculture?

If we truly love God, then we're supposed to love what's on his heart. God's first command to his original creation, Adam and Eve, and Christ's last command to his new creation, the church, are very similar. In Genesis 1:28 (NASB), God commanded Adam and Eve to "be fruitful and multiply, and fill the earth." In Matthew 28:19–20, God commanded his followers to "make disciples of all nations." Both commands require us to spread God's "seed" throughout the earth.

Clearly, our mission isn't to build a Christian subculture. It never has been. Am I against the Christian market? No, not in every case. After all, you are reading a Christian book. There are some good things coming from the market (I'm hoping this book is one of them). But the main question—the main way of measuring the success of our ventures—is whether we're using our influence to transform the world, not just our little Christian corner of it.

But how?

According to Jesus, we're the salt of the earth. Salt has two main functions: it seasons and it preserves.

Salt seasons only when it touches other food. Salt is a preservative only when it infuses something that is in danger of spoiling. Salt is useless when it remains on the shelf or in the shaker. Likewise, we're irrelevant when we separate from the world and refuse to relate with the people in it. When isolated in Christian fortresses, we can't season or preserve the world.

Sometimes our absence from the world is obvious—like when we merely bounce from church activity to church activity. Other times our absence is more subtle—like when we become a member at a Christian workout club. Within that scenario, one more aspect of our lives — our physical health — ends up alienating us from the very people that Jesus asks us to reach.

Jesus tells us to love our neighbors (Matthew 22:39). But it's kind of tough to love our neighbor when we never see our neighbor. We can say we love God, but if we insulate ourselves from people who are hurting, then we're no longer relevant.

Most of us Separatists have the best intentions in rejecting the junk the world produces. Many in our world glorify abuse, greed, violence, injustice, and sexual sin. Feasting on it is hazardous to one's holiness. The world's media aren't all we should be wary of. Purportedly Christian media can present God in an unbiblical way — a serious error because it is masquerading as truth. We should be much stricter about what comes into our minds with the name of Jesus stamped on it than with the music we hear at the mall.

Any media that integrate God are intended to affect and influence the way we think about him. And there are plenty of unorthodox views, teachings, and descriptions of God that come under the Christian label. Such media are a greater danger than blatant secular media because they often go undetected. We tend to drop our defenses when consuming Christian media. We tend to let someone else do our thinking for us. We simply take it all in without bothering to discern what is biblical and what is contrary to it.

A Death Is Inevitable

Referencing God, humanity has always craved a rule book to follow, rather than a relationship to cherish. The nation of Israel was the prototype. God invited them into a unique relationship. They were his special people and he wanted to lead them, but they rejected him. They didn't mind his rules — they just wanted to do everything in their own strength. God eventually gave them some laws through Moses. The purpose of the Law was to reveal their sin, demonstrate their need for God, and make them dependent on him (Galatians 3:21–24).

Only the Israelites didn't follow the plan. When they received the Law, instead of admitting their inability to obey it—instead of asking God for help—they responded arrogantly.

> Then Moses came and recounted to the people all the words of the LORD and all the ordinances; and all the people answered with one voice and said, "All the words which the LORD has spoken *we will do!*"
>
> Exodus 24:3 NASB, emphasis mine

It wasn't long before the Israelites broke their promise. Even though determined, as humans we can only do so much in our own strength.

> They have quickly turned aside from the way which I commanded them. They have made for themselves a molten calf, and have worshiped it, and have sacrificed to it and said, "This is your god, O Israel, who brought you up from the land of Egypt!"
>
> Exodus 32:8 NASB

The Law was never instituted to replace a relationship with God. It was created to increase it. But as history proves often, we miss the heart of the law and embrace the letter of the law instead. This grieves God's heart.

It got so bad at one point in Israel's history that God invited them into a dialogue about the issue. God said, "What are your multiplied sacrifices to Me?... I have had enough of burnt offerings of rams And the fat of fed cattle; And I take no pleasure in the blood of bulls, lambs or goats" (Isaiah 1:11 NASB). The Israelites had all the right actions. We need to give them that. Their deeds were blameless, but they walked away from God somewhere along the way.

Jesus saw the same thing as he walked the earth, and it grieved his heart too. He also invited people into a dialogue by revealing what God truly wanted. Quoting Hosea the prophet, he said, "I desire mercy, not sacrifice" (Matthew 9:13).

God didn't just want their hands; he wanted their hearts as well. But instead of focusing on God, the Israelites focused on rules. Doing so always causes sin to follow, many times in the form of pride. And pride prevents us from ever seeing our need for God. Worse yet, pride always leads to death. It might not always be a physical death—sometimes it's symbolic—but death always makes someone or something a victim. Because of pride, the apostle Paul killed Christians, Simeon Stylites killed his relationship with culture, and the Pharisees killed Christ.

Sometimes pride is so strong it even causes people to kill themselves. In one of my favorite movies, *Les Misérables*, Inspector Javert, played by Geoffrey Rush, does just that. In the last scene this Separatist has a haunting dialogue with the Transformist Jean Valjean, played by Liam Neeson. Rather than humbling himself and admitting his need for help, Inspector Javert takes a strikingly different course. Notice the sad twist of fate in the conversation below:[9]

> *Javert*: You are a difficult problem.
> *Valjean*: Why aren't you taking me in?
> *Javert*: You are my prisoner. Do what I tell you. You don't
> understand the importance of the Law. I have given
> you an order. Obey it. It's a pity the rules don't allow
> me to be merciful. I've tried to live my life without
> breaking a single rule.

In an instant he removes the handcuffs from his captive Valjean and places them upon his own wrists. He then shouts out to Valjean the last words of the entire movie. "You're free!" With that he falls back into the river, drowning himself.

The Transformist goes free while the Separatist dies in a hopeless, shattered attempt at obeying the rules. The message is obvious:

The flesh will do anything, even destroy itself, rather than pursue a relationship with the one who offers salvation.

Your Column

Walking the fine line looks different for every person. God intends for you to wrestle with him through what it means to live in the world, not of the world. This is true especially in those "Christian liberty" issues where there is no standard answer that applies to all people, an idea that Separatists are none too happy about.

"Christian liberty" issues are issues not strictly forbidden in Scripture. There are numerous issues that fall under this category. In Paul's day, some of these were eating food that had been sacrificed to idols, taking a wife, eating only vegetables, and regarding one day above another.

Many of us Separatists want a checklist of dos and don'ts that we can post on our wall. We want a list of rules to nail others with when they don't measure up. There's a nasty monster inside all of us that longs to tell another person, "You failed!" — that relishes knowing there's someone out there who is a little dirtier, a little uglier, and a little more "in need of grace."

God wants more than our checklists. He wants us to grapple with him — to find his strength at the end of ours. He wants us to form our own convictions, not just adopt someone else's. God is just as concerned about the process of establishing your convictions as he is about the convictions you end up holding. And the good news is that our convictions need not involve living atop a fifty-foot column.

CHAPTER 7

THE GIRL BASHERS

Every guy knows the rule.

You can talk about a guy's lack of athleticism, humor, or even intellect, but you *never* disrespect his girlfriend. A couple years ago, I gave in. I broke the rule and bad-mouthed someone else's girl. I was sitting in a coffee shop with a few of my buddies, and we started talking about a guy we all knew. We liked him, a lot. He was our friend. But his girl annoyed the heck out of us, and the negativity started to fly.

Ripping on this girl felt good because it helped to separate us from her. After all, nobody wants to be associated with a loser. And we were clearly associated with her. She had been part of our lives since we were kids. Most of us had even fallen in love with her at one point or another. Maybe that's why we started throwing around the comments — we were insecure or hurt. I walked away from the coffee shop that night feeling pretty low. Although the conversation had been entertaining, I still felt convicted.

But the next week my buddies and I started to talk about our friend's girl again. Only this time it was more intense. Mild dislike soon devolved into hatred. We started telling stories about how this girl offended us. She didn't dress well or talk right. The music she liked was old and stuffy. But our main gripe was her looks. Put simply, she was as ugly as a dog. It was an ugliness that could be seen on the outside and the inside. Her entire look was outdated and irrelevant. She just didn't fit in, and none of us wanted to be around her. We were ashamed to admit that we even knew her, much less that we used to hang out with her.

This went on for several months. And then it got worse. More people knew this girl than I first thought. At parties on the weekends it almost became an opening line—talking about this girl. I met more people than I can remember just by communicating my dislike for her. I had the lines memorized and my timing perfect. People howled as I told story after story about how ridiculous this girl was.

Then I ran into her guy.

I didn't expect to see him. I just kind of bumped into him one day. As soon as I saw him, I realized how much I missed him. I didn't even remember the last time I'd seen him. But my delight quickly changed to deep embarrassment. I could hardly look at him.

He stood and looked me in the eye. "Why, Kary?" he asked quietly. "How could you talk about her like that?"

I could sense how much he loved her, and he could sense how much I hated her. His question bored a hole right through me. Why *did* I hate her so much? What had she ever done to me? Suddenly all my well-rehearsed insults and petty gripes seemed pretty trivial.

I dropped to my knees—I couldn't help it. "Jesus," I said to this guy, "I'm sorry I spoke about your bride, the church, like that."

Are you?

The Toxic Trend

Lots of people are bitter toward the church. Pockets of disenchanted souls gather regularly to complain about how the church has disrespected them. Some of these offenses may have come in the form of legalism, religiosity, or condemnation. Other times it's because she didn't meet their needs exactly right.

Throughout history, the church has been dressed in many different clothes. At times she's relevant and beautiful, adorned in the finest, most elegant apparel. Other times she's in rags, strung out in the gutter of irrelevance.

But to my amazement, Jesus never loses passion for his bride — or for you and me, for that matter. His church holds a special place in his heart and it should in ours too. Christians can't escape the church, so we might as well become reconciled to that fact. After all, when it comes down to it, we *are* the church. Oftentimes we're just expressing our disapproval of *ourselves*.

Perhaps we can have such strong feelings against the church because we approach it with divine expectations. We think that because it's the bride of Christ, it should be perfect, just like Christ. But *it's* not perfect because *we're* not. Yes, there are times when the Father's fingerprints seem to be all over the church, and we feel as though heaven and earth kiss — but a moment later that feeling disappears. Someone does something stupid that rocks us back to reality. Then the church becomes exactly what she is: a gathering of broken people in desperate need of healing.

The church has an uncanny way of getting our hopes up and then leaving us disappointed. Many of us become tempted to avoid the ache rather then embrace it, and so we leave the church and head to the Conformist camp in order to wallow in our wounds. We've been burned by the church and her Separatist tendencies, so it's easier to abandon the idea altogether, to express allegiance to culture rather than to the church.

But do we have to choose between them?

Music artist Moby seems to think so:

In my own strange way, I'm a Christian, in that I really love Christ, and I think that the wisdom of Christ is the highest, strongest wisdom I've ever encountered, and I think that his description of the human condition is about the best description or understanding of the human condition I've ever encountered. And although I try and live my life according to the teachings of Christ, a lot of times I fall short. I wouldn't necessarily consider myself a Christian in the conventional sense of the word, where I go to church or believe in cultural Christianity, but I really do love Christ and recognize him in whatever capacity as I can understand it as God. One of my problems with the church and conventional Christianity is it seems like their focus doesn't have much to do with the teachings of Christ, but rather with their own social agenda. So that's why I tend to be sort of outspoken about how much I dislike conventional cultural Christianity.[1]

Moby raises some good points — some of which I completely agree with. But where does he predominantly go with his angst for the church? The same place Bono has ... outside the church. But can people who claim to follow Christ simply walk out on the church?

Conformists try to. Some of us grew up in Separatist churches, and so our lives are a reaction against our church experience of being taught to retreat from culture. We've vowed never to get sucked into organized religion again. Others of us never fell for Separatist tendencies because our intuitive nature allowed us to see right through the hypocrisy.

All Conformists, out of our desire to be free, believe the church is too restrictive. We want to escape laws, rules, and dead faith. But by alienating ourselves from communities of faith, we end up conforming to culture rather than transforming it. We set our senses on cruise control and feast on everything the world offers, not once thinking about what's tolerable and what's toxic.

Deceived People Lovers

When examining the fine line paradigm in chapter 5, we looked at what it means to live a life of relevance. But all teeter-totters lean toward imbalance. So it is with those of us who lean toward the Conformist camp. Most of us don't have evil motives, but we become unbalanced nonetheless. Notice the pattern below.

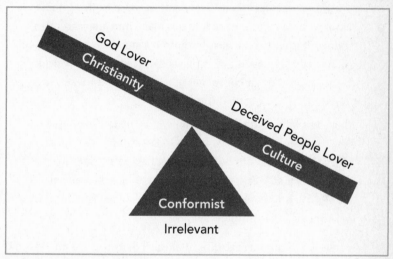

Figure 7.1: The Conformists

We Conformists, like Separatists, are great at justifying our behavior. Where do we get the fuel for our fire? Interestingly enough, from the Bible. We take verses out of context while failing to balance them with the whole of Scripture. Like the Separatists, we approach the Bible with a preconceived grid that allows us to see only what we want to see. Below is some of our often-used ammo:

> For everything God created is good, and nothing is to be
> rejected if it is received with thanksgiving. (1 Timothy 4:4)

Why should my freedom be judged by another's conscience?
(1 Corinthians 10:29)

The earth is the LORD's, and everything in it, the world, and all
who live in it. (Psalm 24:1)

The world is mine, and all that is in it. (Psalm 50:12)

The heavens are yours, and yours also the earth; you founded
the world and all that is in it. (Psalm 89:11)

"Are you so dull?" he asked. "Don't you see that nothing that
enters a man from the outside can make him 'unclean'? For
it doesn't go into his heart but into his stomach, and then out
of his body." (In saying this, Jesus declared all foods "clean.")
He went on: "What comes out of a man is what makes him
'unclean.'" (Mark 7:18–20)

To those not having the law I became like one not having the
law (though I am not free from God's law but am under
Christ's law), so as to win those not having the law. To the
weak I became weak, to win the weak. I have become all
things to all [people] so that by all possible means I might
save some. (1 Corinthians 9:21–22)

Our selective Scripture reading makes us drift toward an extreme
and set up shop in the Conformist camp. Unbalance and irrelevance
soon define our lives.

Characteristics

Those of us who lean toward the Conformist camp are guilty of
certain characteristics. Three of the most common are that we allow
media to replace meditation, liberty to replace love, and tolerance to
replace truth. Let's look at these one at a time.

Few of us take the time to get quiet before God. The average
American is exposed to over three thousand ads every single day.[2]

As a result, keeping our minds biblically and theologically sound is difficult to do. If we're not careful, we can fall into the pattern of being *amused*—not even recognizing the meaning of the word or its impact on our lives. *Amuse* means "to not think." We might benefit by thinking a little bit more about why we don't think.[3]

No one likes to be restricted, especially Conformists. And it's easy to flaunt our freedom without considering how it affects others. We're free in Christ and we want to show it, but not always in the best ways. Some of us have a personal vendetta against Separatists because we barely escaped their grip of control. We enjoy our freedom and vow never to be subjugated to any individual or organization again. But many times we go too far and our freedoms quickly end up enslaving us.

What started as a social drink here and there rapidly evolved into a love affair with hard liquor in order to cope with the stress of life. And what began as watching films that incorporated risqué images somehow transitioned into a steady diet of porn movies.

Truth is true only when it's convenient. Besides, who wants to come off as someone else's judge? As Conformists we certainly don't. Separatists are too narrow and so, instead, we prefer a generous orthodoxy that incorporates anything and everything. In the process, our orthodoxy (meaning "right belief") becomes *any*doxy.

Chameleons of Culture

Conformists sincerely want to be in the world but not of it. We want to be relevant to the world, and we want to be contributors within culture. We want to be defined by what we're for rather than what we're against. The problem is that we're just not sure how to do all this. We experiment with a variety of strategies in order to accomplish these desires, but most of the time we fall far short.

One of our strategies is to show how different we are from typical

Christian stereotypes. We consider ourselves the more "enlightened" ones—and we feel the need to constantly express our disregard for Separatists and the rules they impose. We strive to appear cool and hip to the watching world, desperately distancing ourselves from Separatists. I call this the stereotype strategy.

Other times we resort to what I call the hedonist strategy. We parade our "liberty" for all to see—pushing the line and the limit. We justify our extreme choice of movies and music because we're trying "to become all things to all people." We feast on an endless supply of MTV, rationalizing that we need to know what's going on in the world. It helps us to minister more effectively. We convince ourselves that we consume every form of pleasure because of our love for people. The only problem is that some of these activities we originally engaged in as "tools" for evangelism quickly become addictions.

One other Conformist strategy is what I call the emulating strategy. We set out to think like the world, dress like the world, and act like the world in order to reach the world. The odd thing is that most of the world actually wants something different than itself—and once again we are exposed as irrelevant posers. Although we Conformists claim to value creativity and originality, those of us who embrace this strategy are the most uncreative and unoriginal. We are merely copycats of culture, and the world sees right through our feeble attempts.

These three strategies produce only one thing—irrelevance. Having visited the Conformist camp a time or two, I know the common outcomes. The Bible begins to seem just a tad intolerant in certain places, so we prefer supplemental reading from other walks of spiritualism—in order to relate better to the world, of course. Loving God ends up being reduced to surfing the Net for spiritual topics. And personal convictions become a thing of the past because they only prevent open-mindedness.

Separatists are fueled by a fear of not being holy. Conformists are fueled by a fear of not being accepted by the world. Yet in our quest for "relevance" we become the opposite. Because culture is always changing, we're always changing. As a result, we're in an eternal identity crisis. We're never quite sure who we are or what we believe, so we end up doing what comes easiest: conforming to culture rather than transforming it.

Forsaking the Assembly

Most of us Conformists don't trust "organized religion." Some of us would even go so far as to say that we hate it. We don't see the need for a community of faith. If asked, we might not admit it. But our absence from church communicates what we truly believe.

Withdrawing from the church seems like a new fad, but it's as old as the church itself. The writer of the book of Hebrews warned people in his day, "Let us not give up meeting together, as some are in the habit of doing, but let us encourage one another—and all the more as you see the Day approaching" (Hebrews 10:25).

Don't get me wrong: I understand why people give up on the church; I just don't agree with it. At one point in my life I became disillusioned with the church as well. I saw its gossip groups, its legalism, and its petty rule-based religiosity. I attended out of duty for several months.

Then I decided to stop being part of the problem. I had a change of mind. I decided to stop looking at my own needs and how I felt that the church was not meeting them. Instead, I focused on those around me. I ended up meeting a number of other wounded people who were just as tired and fed up as I was.

I listened and heard their stories. I gained courage as I observed their courage. What excited me most was watching how they transcended their frustration. Mike and Mindi started a house church network in Columbus. Will became a missionary in Ireland. Sarah wrote a book called *Dear Church: Letters from a Disillusioned Generation*. John cofounded Asia's Hope, an international missions effort committed to opening orphanages, student centers, and Christian schools. Catherine joined a sorority in order to stretch her faith and live it out before her new sisters. Nate, Ezra, Keith, John, Mike, Drew, Matt, and Andy founded Driven, a young adult conference committed to gathering a generation to become catalysts for Christ within church and culture. Mark and Jennifer started the Landing Place, a community of faith in Columbus's Short North. And the list of my heroes goes on and on.

Yes, the church has flaws. After all, I'm part of it. If the only church around is full of legalistic Separatists, then my advice is to separate from the Separatists.

Start your own church.

Why not? We need to stop criticizing and making excuses.

Jesus' disciples transformed the world, and they were only in their late teens and early twenties.

I take that back. "Transformed" is an understatement. They flipped the world on its head, and we're still feeling the effects today.

Stay optimistic. Every Christ-follower needs a community of faith. These communities probably look a lot different than the traditional church some of us grew up attending. They don't need to meet in a church building or have a fixed order of service. Keep your eyes open for them; don't give up on joining a community of like-minded Christ-followers.

I'm afraid that if we former churchgoers can't enter a process of healing, move through our pain, and convert our energies into something constructive, an entire generation might accomplish nothing more than sitting around and complaining about the church's irrelevance.

Needs Matter

So why, considering all its problems, am I sold on the church?

For starters, Jesus is. It's his bride, and if I'm not passionate about her, then I'm not in tune with him. But it's more than that. We've been uniquely created to have some of our needs met through a community of faith. Just like a marriage relationship, our needs aren't met by insisting on them. No, they're met in the process of relationship. But in relationships many people start by asking the wrong question. We demand to know, "How do you plan on meeting *my* needs?"

We often approach the church with the same needy question. This phenomenon — called "consumer church" — is pervasive. It means that when our needs aren't met, we just pick up and leave. Sounds like a lot of marriages to me. But when we approach the church with the opposite mind-set — of serving others — strangely, in the end, we're the ones who are served. Our needs get met.

What are some of those needs? Besides the obvious ones like food, clothing, and shelter, studies show that humans have three common core needs.[4] Although researchers may label them differently, they are essentially purpose, community, and transcendence. Providentially, these three needs are meant to be met within the context of a local church. When we exercise our spiritual gifts in the service of others, we find purpose; when we make ourselves accountable to a group of people who care about us, we discover community; and when we encourage other believers in the midst of their personal battles, we bump up against transcendence.

Exercising Spiritual Gifts

We all want to belong — to know that we're needed. But many times, when it comes to our place in the church, we feel like extras.

Why is this? The church is supposed to be interdependent — made up of individuals who together make something beautiful, Christ's body (Romans 12:5). Because we're each unique, we have a unique contribution that's critical for the overall health of the body. So when we're absent, the whole body suffers.

Imagine a day without your eyes or your ears or your legs. Very soon you'd notice your body part was missing. You'd notice what you could no longer do. Without your eyes you could no longer see. Without your ears you could no longer hear.

It's the same with us and our community of faith. When we're gone, people should notice that our unique gift is missing. If our unique gift is compassion, then the body should notice itself lacking tenderness. If our unique gift is administration, then the body should notice less organization.

Sadly, many of our churches wouldn't notice our absence. We could be gone for months or years and there would be no void. They wouldn't miss us because many of us don't contribute anything. We just sit and soak.

No wonder we don't feel the *need* for church. It's because the church doesn't *need* us. When we approach church merely for what we'll get out of it and not what we can put into it, then sooner or later we'll be disappointed. We each have a significant gift of grace, and our need for purpose is realized within the context of serving others. As Peter reminds us, "Each one should use whatever gift he has received to serve others, faithfully administering God's grace in its various forms" (1 Peter 4:10).

Accountability with One Another

Relationship is an overused word. It's used to describe everything from an intimate affair ("They had a relationship") to a casual contract ("He has a relationship with State Farm"). This makes it tough to define what real relationship is. Within the context of our dialogue, real relationship always includes accountability.

Accountability demands that we take off our masks. There's nothing as scary as doing this in the presence of someone because that person can reject us. No wonder so many of us flee from authenticity. But there's nothing more freeing than taking off our masks because, perhaps for the first time, the other person can choose to accept us for *who we really are.*

When we avoid accountability, we avoid community, one of our three core needs. Worse yet, we set ourselves up to fail, and we invite hypocrisy into our hearts. There's nothing biblical about doing life on our own. In the creation story, isolation was the only thing God wasn't happy with: "It is not good for the man to be alone" (Genesis 2:18).

Community is the answer for isolation. It's also the antidote for hypocrisy.

Accountability promotes integrity. It gives those who have our best interests in mind permission to ask questions about how we're honestly doing in our marriages, friendships, thought life, devotional life, prayer life, and life itself. Our need for community is realized within the context of accountability. "As iron sharpens iron, so one [friend] sharpens another" (Proverbs 27:17).

Encouragement of Believers

In the fifth century, Philo of Alexandria said, "Be kind, for everyone you meet is fighting a great battle." He recognized life was not a series of random disconnected events, but rather that we all play a role in this cosmic metanarrative. When we choose to live within this reality, we experience transcendence—excelling beyond the normal limits of existence.

Life is bigger than the little world inside our heads. With this in mind, we all have a critical responsibility to help others in their battle. This is what encouragement means—implanting courage—equipping others with the necessary strength to face their upcoming battles.[5] And when those around us battle well, we tend to be more courageous in our own battles—because as Christ-followers we're all connected.

Fear threatens to sabotage, and when we cultivate fear, we give it the chance to do what it does best: paralyze. Fear seeks to immobilize us—to keep us from doing much of anything. We'll never get to the place where we eradicate fear. That's okay. "Courage is not the absence of fear, but rather the judgement that something else is more important than fear."[6]

Local churches provide us with the context to encourage other Christ-followers. Our words of encouragement breathe fresh air into weary souls.[7] These words can be in the form of prayers, stories, compliments, or the Word of God itself. We bump up against transcendence when we encourage others.

> Encourage the exhausted, and strengthen the feeble.
> Say to those with anxious heart,
>> "Take courage, fear not.
>> Behold, your God will come with vengeance;
>> The recompense of God will come,
>> But He will save you."
>
> Isaiah 35:3–4 NASB

What about Conformist Churches?

Conformist churches may be a rarer breed than Separatist churches, but they do exist. Often the trend in Conformist churches is to blindly infuse humanistic ideals, secular philosophies, and antibiblical worldviews into the DNA of the church.

When we turn our affections from Christ to anything or anyone else, we engage in spiritual adultery. This was common in the Old Testament. Israel regularly blended worship of the true God with worship of false gods. Believers in the New Testament were guilty of this as well. Because of this, the apostle Paul jealously fought for the purity of the church. He wanted to present her spotless to her bridegroom, Jesus Christ. He strove to preach a pure gospel with pure doctrines, and the preservation and proclamation of this gospel became Paul's life mission.

> I am jealous for you with a godly jealousy. I promised you to one husband, to Christ, so that I might present you as a pure virgin to him. But I am afraid that just as Eve was deceived by the serpent's cunning, your minds may somehow be led astray from your sincere and pure devotion to Christ. For if someone comes to you and preaches a Jesus other than the Jesus we preached, or if you receive a different spirit from the one you received, or a different gospel from the one you accepted, you put up with it easily enough.
>
> 2 Corinthians 11:2−4

We would do well to keep these verses close to our hearts. If we're honest, as Conformists we don't have a reputation for being the most discerning individuals. Often, we slowly let other doctrines seep in — believing the Jesus of the Bible is a little too extreme. Some of his words lean toward exclusivity, and so we pay less and less attention to certain verses and ignore others altogether.

Tragically we end up embracing an extrabiblical or antibiblical Jesus. A. W. Tozer, in *The Knowledge of the Holy*, labeled this tendency for what it is, idolatry:

> The idolatrous heart assumes that God is other than He is — in itself a monstrous sin — and substitutes for the true God one made after its own likeness. The essence of idolatry is the entertainment of thoughts about God that are unworthy of Him.[8]

God doesn't give us the luxury of approaching him on our own terms. In the Old Testament, when people did, it meant judgment, discipline, and even death. We observe this in Cain's offering, Saul's sacrifice, and Nadab's strange fire.[9] Each of these examples shows how people thought they could come to God in their own way. God didn't classify these actions as innocent misunderstandings but as attempts at intentional idolatry. Tozer continues:

> If we insist upon trying to imagine Him, we end up with an idol, made not with hands, but with thoughts; and an idol of the mind is as offensive to God as an idol of the hand. Left to ourselves, we tend immediately to reduce God to manageable terms. We want a god we can control. We need the feeling of security that comes from knowing what God is like.[10]

These "idols" of the mind must be destroyed. We'll never be relevant when we allow them to be erected within our lives. If we do idolize earthly things, then we have nothing to offer the world because we're exactly like it.

And not everything in this world is neutral. For example, God tells us that within this world, demons are seeking to influence our thinking. We usually shrug this off in light of our Western worldview. The whole spiritual dimension ranks right up there with elves and unicorns. But let's not be fooled. "In later times some will fall away from the faith, paying attention to deceitful spirits and doctrines of demons" (1 Timothy 4:1 NASB). Lest we forget, we're in a battle, and this one isn't against flesh and blood. We're wise to set our attention and affections on modeling ourselves after biblical principles and practices.

Our Enemy comes cleverly undetected, not in a red suit with a pitchfork. He subtly seduces the church away from the truth and, creating a toxic blend, he mixes truth with error. The Bible predicted this reality:

> The time will come when they will not endure sound doctrine; but wanting to have their ears tickled, they will accumulate for

themselves teachers in accordance to their own desires, and will turn away their ears from the truth.

2 Timothy 4:3–4 NASB

In light of these dangers, it's easy to overreact and tip to the other irrelevant extreme—the Separatist camp. As always, unbalance is only a breath away.

I hope you won't misinterpret me. Here's what I'm *not* saying:

- That we shouldn't be creative.
- That we can't learn from what the world has to offer.
- That we shouldn't adjust our methodology.

Take a moment to understand a little more about what these statements suggest.

We Must Be Creative

The last thing we need is more boring, static churches or individuals who present a prepackaged, demystified understanding of God. The people of God must continue to create. We must explore, discuss, and imagine what it looks like to follow Christ in the world in which we live. We must join God in a transformational journey as he reveals himself. Of course we should be wary of idolatry of the mind, but we must commit to not only being students of the Word but also students of the world.

We tend to forget that God's first act was to create. The universe is his canvas. He didn't have to use color or taste, but he did. He didn't have to create picoplankton—part of the aquatic ecosystem, but so tiny that 500,000 large ones fit on the head of a pin—but he did. We, the church, should be the most creative people on the planet. If God is *the* Creator, and if we're created in his image, then why wouldn't we also be hardwired to create?

But for some reason we've gotten comfortable killing this part of who we are. We've been taught to ignore the artist within. In his book *Orbiting the Giant Hairball: A Corporate Fool's Guide to Surviving with Grace*, author Gordon MacKenzie lets us into this reality. He tells about a frequent experience with the elementary students who attend his creativity workshops. He asks his first grade classes how many of them are artists. All raise their hands with great enthusiasm. When he asks second graders, about 50 percent raise their hands. In third grade, it's ten out of thirty. And in sixth grade, only one or two students, timidly at this age, admit to being artists.[11]

Why the change? Maybe creativity scares us. Maybe we feel insecure with too many variables — craving boundaries instead. Maybe we believe creativity will be critiqued and criticized, and we're reluctant to put anything out there, fearful of being evaluated. Regardless, the outcome is the same. We stop creating, and when we do, we deny a large part of what makes us human. We must transcend these fears, partner with God, and join him in cocreating. The church must be the forerunner, setting the pace for what it looks like to create and be creative.

We Must Learn from What the World Has to Offer

We have dual citizenship — a home here on earth as well as in heaven (Philippians 3:20). We're supposed to live and move and work within this present world. If the world discovers something redemptive, why do we often fear incorporating it?

I think it's because we forget who our enemy is. We think it's the world and so we feel the need to try to escape it. But our enemy isn't the world. "Our struggle is not against flesh and blood, but against the rulers, against the authorities, against the powers of this dark world and against the spiritual forces of evil in the heavenly realms" (Ephesians 6:12). When we live as though we should escape the world, we actually embrace an unbiblical ideology. God inspired the

Bible and he inspired the world. The two shouldn't be pitted against one another. God's first book (creation) harmonizes with God's second book (Scripture), since he is the author of both.

We can and should exegete the world, mining it for its redeeming resources, principles, and paradigms. We should filter these findings through a biblical worldview, embracing what's profitable and rejecting what's problematic. All truth is God's truth and the entire world is his. When the world "discovers" something true, they're merely uncovering God's handiwork. We should invite these discoveries—whether they be penicillin, biofuels, solar energy, or space travel—rather than feel threatened by them.

We Must Adjust Our Methodology

Some aspects of Christianity are fluid and others are fixed. Some aspects of our faith should change and others must always remain the same.

God never changes. He's the same yesterday, today, and forever. But you and I are always changing, sometimes even from one minute to the next. How do we know what things should stay constant and what things should remain changeable?

As Conformists we get into trouble when we begin changing theology in order to accommodate the needs of culture. When we bend the doctrine of salvation in order to include paths to God other than Jesus, a practice quite frequent today, then the church loses its relevance.

Although our individual understanding of God may change within this life, we're the ones who change, not God. For Conformists, almost everything is up for grabs. So many issues are on the table that there are few fixed truths. Author Gene A. Getz clarifies the issue by creating a distinction between what should change and what shouldn't. He uses two terms: function and form. Functions are "activities that believers engage in to meet certain spiritual needs and to reach certain goals in order to carry out biblical commands and directives."[12] Functions are things like preaching, teaching, worship, and evangelism. These things don't change. The function of evangelism has been around since the birth of the church. We're not given the luxury of deciding whether we want to incorporate or redefine it.

But our forms must change. Forms are "patterns, methodologies, means, and techniques that are created to carry out biblical functions and directives."[13] Our form of evangelism must change. And so it has. Throughout history the church has adjusted the way it shares faith with others—ranging from knocking door-to-door, making contacts, friendship evangelism, rallies, discussion groups, classes, service projects, debates, and open-air events. Culture changed and so did our forms.

Shockingly, in recent years some extreme Conformists began changing functions as well as forms. They established themselves and their experience, rather than God's Word, as the authority. They, rather than God, decide which functions to keep and which ones to do away with. They redefine functions in their own words and in their own way. Instead of living on the fine line, they cross the line—and so lose themselves, not to mention their relevance.

Nonconformists Are Nonexistent

Several years ago, I was chatting with a guy about the fine line paradigm. For the sake of illustration, I'll call him Tom. I didn't know him well, but as we spoke I could tell he was upset. His story unfolded, and it was obvious that for some reason he was ticked at the church. He had some serious wounds.

I asked Tom if he felt like he struggled with Separatist or Conformist tendencies. I was sincerely trying to understand Tom and his wounds better. I was surprised by his response. Tom proudly said, "I'm neither. I'm a nonconformist. I march to my own beat."

As he told me his life story, it seemed like he had Conformist tendencies. So I wasn't sure if, in drafting the fine line paradigm, I hadn't factored in this "nonconformist" camp.

I asked him to tell me more. It became apparent that he was a Conformist. He admitted that recently he had been ignoring God's Word. He confessed that the last few months he focused on promoting his liberty rather than exercising his love for others.

I spent some more time thinking about Tom. As I systematically reviewed his situation, it became clear that he wasn't a nonconformist. He was just a Conformist with a bruised ego.

Here's why:

From an early age, we're indoctrinated to do what is right in our own eyes. Strangely, we're expected to conform to nonconformity. Ironically, in striving to be nonconformists, we actually become Conformists. Wrapped in the cloak of individuality, nonconformists deceive themselves into thinking they're different from all the rest. But a glance around a high school lunchroom will make abundantly clear that this is conformity in its truest sense.

From the outside, nonconformists seem extremely accommodating and accepting. But any deviation from tolerance soon causes the nonconformist to become extremely intolerant. Tom revealed himself with his own words. By identifying himself as a radical nonconformist, he revealed what he truly was — a Conformist.

But there is an alternative. And that alternative is growing.

PART III

WHAT SHOULD WE DO?

Be not afraid of growing slowly;
be afraid only of standing still.
Chinese Proverb

CHAPTER 8

ORANGE CONSTRUCTION CONES

The image makes even the most skilled driver white-knuckle the wheel. Carefree cruising is exchanged for tension-filled travel when we spot one of those notorious lines of orange construction cones.

Weather conditions can be ideal. Perhaps the autumn breeze is ruffling the leaves of the fire-colored trees that line the interstate. The sky is clear, passengers are content. You might even have an iPod full of your favorite tunes and a cooler full of your favorite snacks. You might be resting in a leather seat with lumbar levers supporting your back. Yet all it takes is a few of those orange construction cones to ruin the trip.

The sight of those cones can cause an anxiety attack because it usually means our journey will be delayed and often for way too long. Sitting still is simply unacceptable. I think there's something deep inside us that reacts negatively to remaining in the same place. We don't want to stay stationary, held against our will, when we're trying to get somewhere.

As humans we want progress. We want movement. We want change, even if it's just a change in scenery. But orange construction cones are the enemy of change, and so we sit and sulk.

Camps without Change

Separatists and Conformists don't realize it, but they love orange construction cones. They don't want movement, and they're quite content to stay exactly where they are. It gives them a sense of comfort, of familiarity, of control. On the road of life, they'd rather take a nap in the rest stop.

This desire for immobility opposes God's heart because the Bible is all about life change. It's why Jesus came — in order to bring change to every person. Change is available to us as long as we hold an open hand out to God (Philippians 1:6; 2 Corinthians 3:18).

While driving my car the other day, I saw a message on one of those church marquees. Don't worry — this was actually a good one. It said, "God loves us just the way we are, but he loves us too much to leave us that way."

I liked it because it reminded me that, as believers, we must stop thinking that the need for change is only for unbelievers. Rather, as followers of Christ, our lives should continually be marked with change. It's what we signed up for. Change always involves a death of sorts. That's why we fear it. Change can mean the death of an idea, a tradition, a grudge, or a preference. Although salvation is the ultimate change, and a death of the old nature, this present life can and should be a constant process of deaths and rebirths. The ultimate death is when we refuse to change — when we settle for obeying the orange construction cones and remain in one place forever.

Separatists and Conformists do exactly this. They resist change. Separatists are stuck as deceived God lovers, immobilized in their loyalty to Christianity. And Conformists are stuck as deceived people lovers, immobilized in their loyalty to culture.

There is only one way to get the church back on the highway: enter the Transformist.

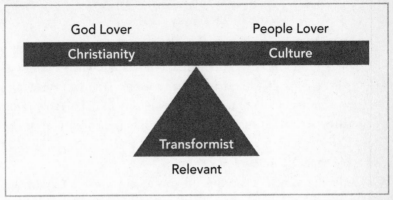

Figure 8.1: The Transformists

Transformists are the alternative, the exception, the remnant. Transformists are people in paradox, people living in the world but not of the world. Their lives are characterized by balance and relevance.

Although the Transformists' teeter-totter is balanced now, it won't be for long. Unlike Separatists who embrace only Christianity or Conformists who embrace only culture, Transformists embrace both.

Transformists actually *invite* tension because they know that where there's tension, there's life and growth. But most importantly, where there's growth, there's Jesus. By inviting tension, we invite Jesus.

Separatists don't need Jesus—they have everything figured out. And Conformists don't need Jesus—they say anything goes.

Transformists are different. They know they can't do it on their own, which is the exact realization that precedes Jesus showing up to help us. Jesus reveals himself as the teeter-totter moves up and down, as Transformists struggle to balance Christianity with culture and loving God with loving people. This is the way to relevance.

First-Century Cones

Early in his life, the apostle Paul would have loved orange construction cones—he wasn't too thrilled about change. Jewish religious leaders weren't exactly known as cutting edge. Tradition ruled, and they were more than upset by the upsetting actions of the rabbi Jesus. Rising from the dead tends to shatter a few treasured preconceptions, and the Jewish leaders could feel their control slipping away as people began to follow Jesus.

For Paul, the avid Separatist, life was all about a dutiful religious performance. Adding to God's Word and insulating himself from people characterized his life. But Jesus changed all that on one ordinary day on the road to Damascus. Paul fought back, but Jesus won, and we did too.

Here's why: Like any good Separatist, Paul wanted to silence the convicting cries of the Transformists who surrounded him. They wrecked his religion, so Paul wrecked them. He killed followers of Christ in an attempt to kill Christianity. In a strange twist, Christianity ended up killing him—at least the Separatist in him.

The writer Luke introduces us to Paul, originally named Saul, and his hatred for followers of Jesus. We first meet Paul in the book of Acts right in the middle of a bloody scene. He and his fellow Separatists are about to kill Stephen, who would soon become the first martyr for Jesus.

> And Saul was there, giving approval to [Stephen's] death. On that day a great persecution broke out against the church at Jerusalem, and all except the apostles were scattered throughout Judea and Samaria. Godly men buried Stephen and mourned deeply for him. But Saul began to destroy the church. Going from house to house, he dragged off men and women and put them in prison.
>
> Acts 8:1–3

Saul continued his destructive spree. He stepped up the intensity by asking the high priest for letters that would give him permission to imprison any follower of Jesus. He couldn't stand Transformists, so he got a license to kill them — literally.

But on the road to Damascus, he met Jesus, the original Transformist. In a bright light Jesus confronted him with a piercing question, "Saul, Saul, why do you persecute me?" (Acts 9:4). At first Saul didn't recognize Jesus. He became temporarily blind and wandered for three days in this condition. It might have been symbolic of the spiritual blindness that had defined his life up until that point.

But then another Transformist, Ananias, laid his hands on Saul and said, "Brother Saul, the Lord — Jesus, who appeared to you on the road as you were coming here — has sent me so that you may see again and be filled with the Holy Spirit." The Bible records that "immediately, something like scales fell from Saul's eyes, and he could see again. He got up and was baptized, and after taking some food, he regained his strength. Saul spent several days with the disciples in Damascus. At once he began to preach in the synagogues that Jesus is the Son of God" (Acts 9:17–20).

Paul changed from being a Separatist to a Transformist in a dramatic fashion. Immediately, he began to share this message of hope with others. He wouldn't stop until he drew his last breath. Paul would become one of the most relevant people who ever lived — even though originally he could have been the poster child for the Separatist camp. But maybe that's what made him such a vibrant Transformist. His irrelevant extremes were exposed in a public way, and he was constantly reminded what Jesus saved him from.

After his conversion, Paul didn't pursue relevance. Instead, he pursued Jesus. But by pursuing Jesus, he naturally became relevant. And as long as he kept following Jesus, he was relevant.

Notice what this Transformist wrote about himself: "I have become all things to all [people] so that by all possible means I might save some" (1 Corinthians 9:22). On the surface this seems a bit un-balanced — like someone who doesn't know who he is — like a social chameleon or a Conformist. But then Paul explains,

> I do not run like a man running aimlessly; I do not fight like a man beating the air. No, I beat my body and make it my slave so that after I have preached to others, I myself will not be disqualified for the prize.
>
> 1 Corinthians 9:26–27

This seems unbalanced too — like someone who adds to God's Word — like someone consumed with personal holiness and rules. Sounds like a Separatist.

But Paul was neither. He walked the fine line and avoided the Separatist and Conformist camps. Paul maintained a pure conscience while participating in culture. Paul balanced his love for God with his love for people. He depicted one who lived in the world but was not of it.

But how?

Road Trip

Paul wasn't a novice when it came to knowing God's Word. After his preliminary education, he was sent to the premier Jewish school of sacred learning in Jerusalem to become a rabbi. There, as a pupil of Rabbi Gamaliel, he "was thoroughly trained in the law."[1] He dialogued regularly with the religiously educated of his day. Tradition tells us that he may have been a member of the Great Sanhedrin, the equivalent of the Supreme Court in the ancient Jewish court system.[2] Because of this, he knew the Law in an intimate way.

As a lifelong learner, Paul was always increasing his knowledge (Acts 9:22). Following his conversion, he spent at least three years in the Arabian Desert studying the person Jesus, the one he once persecuted.[3]

Paul wasn't a novice when it came to the world either. His hometown, Tarsus, "surpassed all other universities, such as Alexandria and Athens, in the study of philosophy and educational literature in general."[4] Tarsus was an integrated city, a melting pot—with music, culture, and literature from many parts of the world. Scholars believe that "as a citizen of Tarsus, Paul was a citizen of the whole world."[5]

Paul, a Transformist, knew God and the Scriptures. Paul, a Transformist, knew people and their culture. He was committed to both without compromising either.

Although many examples from the Bible show Paul embodying the life of a Transformist, his visit to Athens is particularly noteworthy. The city was consumed with idolatry. A Roman satirist saying was that it was "easier to find a god at Athens than a man."[6]

Paul arrived in Athens earlier than his colleagues Silas and Timothy, but he didn't waste any time. If Paul were a Conformist, he would have taken advantage of the opportunity to mindlessly consume Greek culture. Without the accountability of his fellow missionaries, Paul could have rationalized feasting on all Athens had to offer.

If Paul were a Separatist, he would have done what Separatists do—separate. Paul would have checked into his hotel, ordered room service, and caught up on his latest religious reading. He would have talked himself out of visiting the sites of Athens for fear of sinning.

But Paul was a Transformist, so he didn't do either. Instead, he began to transform the culture. He didn't hide from the culture—but moved within it. He didn't see culture as the enemy—but took his faith into the marketplace. He didn't digest the culture—but discerned it. He studied the people within it, discovering their intricacies in order to transform them with a life-changing message. Daily he reasoned with the Jews, the God-fearing Gentiles, and anyone else who happened to be present (Acts 17:17). He preached about the Lord Jesus Christ and the resurrection (Acts 17:18).

Soon the city was buzzing with talk of a strange preacher who preached strange gods. The Athenians took Paul to the philosophical hot spot of the day, called the Areopagus.

The Areopagus, or Mars Hill, was the location of pagan temples where philosophers gathered each day to discuss, argue, and learn new ideas. Paul, the Transformist who loved God and people, the man who connected his Christianity with his culture, spoke a relevant message that his listeners could comprehend. He gained favor with his audience by acknowledging their spirituality: "[People] of Athens! I see that in every way you are very religious" (Acts 17:22).

He demonstrated his knowledge of their culture by quoting two Greek poets, Epimenides ("in him we live and move and have our being") and Aratus of Soli ("we are ... his offspring").[7]

Paul learned their culture, their literature, their common places, their marketplaces, and their holy places. He understood the city's layout, the city's philosophy, and the city's religion. He gained all that knowledge *about* the people, motivated by his love *for* the people, before mentioning one word about God.

Paul was incredibly accommodating, but when the time came, he stood his ground. He said, "What you worship in ignorance, this I proclaim to you" (Acts 17:23 NASB). Although Paul acknowledged their spirituality, he also addressed their ignorance. When he spoke to them about God, he didn't hold back—knowing that identifying with their culture could only bring him so far. It could gain him common ground, but it couldn't make dead people become alive or sinners become saints. The Athenians needed to meet Jesus.

So Paul proceeded to introduce them to the God who made everything, the God who gives life, the God who ordains the position of people, the God who judges people, and the God who raised his Son from the dead.

He didn't get applause. But this Transformist remained true to the message and the mission. He used culture and enjoyed culture without being compromised by it—all while embodying the gospel to his audience.

Audiences typically respond to Transformists with criticism, curiosity, or conversion. The Mars Hill crowd was no different. Some criticized and made fun of this Jewish preacher. Others were interested in hearing his strange message again. And a few actually were converted. These few were transformed by Jesus. The Bible tells us "some of the people became followers of Paul and believed. Among them was Dionysius, a member of the Areopagus, also a woman named Damaris, and a number of others" (Acts 17:34 TNIV).

Some of these believers probably lived a fairly simple life after they became Transformists. But church history tells us a different story about one of them. According to Eusebius, the Father of Church History, Dionysius later became the bishop of the church at Athens.[8] What began as a seed planted in a transformational dialogue bloomed, one day, into a citywide church.[9] We never know what God might do in and through us.

It Must Have Been Love

Paul's actions were *centered on* and *motivated by* his love for God and people. Relevance defined him and his strategy for sharing his faith. But if love is so powerful, why does it often seem so weak? Maybe the reason why love seems trite is that we need to grow in our understanding of what love is. Maybe we need to learn, and relearn, what it means to love God with all our heart, soul, and mind and to love our neighbor as ourselves. Maybe love is much more than we give it credit for.

CHAPTER 9

SKIN-DEEP LOVE

How many parts make up a person?

In the school of medicine, the right answer might be 206, referring to the number of bones in the human body, or 600, referring to the number of muscles.

But in the school of religion, things get trickier. Theologians have suggested that humans are one-, two-, or even three-part creatures. So how many parts are we? Who knows? More importantly, who cares?[1]

God knows, but I don't think he cares — at least not about how many parts we are. What he *does* care about is how we love him with the parts we have, be it one, two, three, or two hundred or six hundred.

Jesus quoted Moses to show the importance of the command to love. But you'd think that Jesus would have quoted Moses correctly. Moses said, "Love the LORD your God with all your heart and with all your soul and with all your *strength*" (Deuteronomy 6:5, emphasis mine). Jesus said, "Love the Lord your God with all your heart and with all your soul and with all your *mind*" (Matthew 22:37, emphasis mine).

How odd. This is a big verse — a *really* big one. Jesus said it was so important that "all the Law and the prophets hang on" this command.[2] But if it's that critical, why didn't he quote it correctly?

The point is, I don't think he got it wrong. I think Jesus was emphasizing that we must love God with all our parts, not that we should get hung up on how many parts we have. He was telling us to love God connectedly.

A disconnected love for God prevents us from becoming Transformists. When we love God with only a part of ourselves, it's impossible to be relevant. Sadly, many of us don't know any better.

The Connection

Only in recent times have we begun to catch up to the brilliance of Jesus' teaching about interconnectivity. We can thank the Greeks for our confusion. Dating back to ancient Greece, philosophers viewed the world as a conflict between the material and the immaterial, the natural and the spiritual.[3] They compartmentalized these two entities, even labeling the material as bad.

These two parts of a person, the material and the immaterial, were thought to be separate and distinct. René Descartes, the seventeenth-century philosopher, split the body and mind even farther apart — "I *think*, therefore I am."

In our time, science and medicine have partnered to prove the Greeks and Descartes dead wrong. People can't be fragmented into different, independent segments. The body, soul, mind, and every other part of us are interconnected. We can't love God with our actions but not with our words. We can't love him with our time but not with our talent. When we do, we don't love God completely. And when we don't love God completely, it's difficult to be relevant because relevance is all about loving God holistically and loving our neighbor as ourselves.

Let's say you're about to have a nice chat with a friend over coffee and bagels. You're both in the kitchen getting the cups, plates, and coffee ready. As you pour the coffee into two mugs, your friend turns suddenly and bumps you. You spill the scalding liquid all over your hand. You feel the skin on your hand flare up immediately. You yell in pain and spit a rude word at your friend. In agony you run cold water across your tender hand.

But very soon other things will need your attention. Not only are you suffering physical pain but you probably have some emotional pain to deal with too. And if you sinned in your anger, you and God will need to have a talk as well. You see how connected our lives are as body-soul-spirit creatures? We're complete people who were never meant to be fragmented.

Sometimes we wish our spirituality could be just *part* of our lives instead of our whole life. We wish loving God and others affected only some of our schedule rather than our entire calendar. But we weren't made to turn spirituality off and on or to love God and others only part of the time. God intends for us to have unified lives in which our love for him and others permeates all of who we are and all of what we do.

We have a tough time understanding this, but the Hebrews didn't. They understood we are connected creatures. For them there was no dualism. The human writers of the New Testament wrote from this mind-set as well.

Jesus certainly taught this unity. We see this played out in his darkest hour. Jesus didn't condemn the disciples because they forsook him. Rather, he understood the link between the body and soul, and he knew their physical weariness contributed to their spiritual weariness.

"'Could you men not keep watch with me for one hour?' he asked Peter. 'Watch and pray so that you will not fall into temptation. The spirit is willing, but the body is weak'" (Matthew 26:40–41).

No matter how much the disciples wanted to remain awake and

pray, they couldn't. In this case, their spirits were enslaved by their bodies. Exhausted, they couldn't disconnect from this reality.

Dangers of Disconnection

When we love God with only part of ourselves, we love him incompletely. And when we love him incompletely we're flirting with irrelevance.

The rationale is fairly simple: The more connected our love for God is, the more our lives are marked by relevance. The reverse is true as well: The more fragmented our love for God is, the more our lives will be marked by irrelevance.

Many of us say we love God, but we love him only partially. We love him at times with our heart, at times with our soul, at times with our mind. But most of us fail to love God completely in an interconnected manner. This hinders our ability to live as Transformists, because disconnected love is offensive. Disconnected love prevents us from realizing how unhealthy we are.

Disconnected Love Is Offensive and Insincere

At certain times in Israel's history the people had a disconnected "love" for God. It was insincere and manufactured. They had all the right actions—presenting various sacrifices and offerings to the Lord—but he could see beneath their skin-deep love:

> Hear the word of the LORD, you rulers of Sodom; listen to the law of our God, you people of Gomorrah! "The multitude of your sacrifices—what are they to me?" says the LORD. "I have more than enough of burnt offerings, of rams and the fat of fattened animals; I have no pleasure in the blood of bulls and lambs and goats. When you come to appear before me, who has asked this of you, this trampling of my courts? Stop bringing meaning-

less offerings! Your incense is detestable to me. New Moons, Sabbaths and convocations — I cannot bear your evil assemblies. Your New Moon festivals and your appointed feasts my soul hates. They have become a burden to me; I am weary of bearing them. When you spread out your hands in prayer, I will hide my eyes from you; even if you offer many prayers, I will not listen. Your hands are full of blood; wash and make yourselves clean. Take your evil deeds out of my sight! Stop doing wrong, learn to do right! Seek justice, encourage the oppressed. Defend the cause of the fatherless, plead the case of the widow."

Isaiah 1:10–17

The Israelites didn't seem to mind their insincerity. They managed to cast a few token acts of kindness God's way in order to keep him off their backs, but they were just going through the motions. Their hearts weren't in it, and he knew.

God knows everything, including when we're faking it. So why do we try to placate him and pretend we're not? Transformists aren't imposters. They can't be. Relevance can happen only when we're real. Insincerity may seem like a subtle footnote, but it's actually a violent attack on our potential to be Transformists. God sees through our façade and, if we're honest, people do too.

Disconnected Love Prevents Us from Realizing How Unhealthy We Are

Nothing is more frustrating than people who are sick but won't admit it. A doctor can examine us and determine that we're sick. Test results can medically confirm it. Still, if we don't acknowledge this fact, then chances are we're not going to get better. It takes humility to admit that we're sick and in need of healing.

Disconnected love has the tendency to fool us and those around us. It makes us think we're healthy when we're really not. Wearing a convincing mask, the Pharisees thought they were pretty healthy too. When Jesus showed up and told them they were sick, they didn't acknowledge it. Instead, they told him that *he* was the sick one. Their pride prevented them from seeing their need to be healed.

David's Dilemma

Why do so many of us settle for a disconnected love and follow in the footsteps of the Pharisees? Why do most people, both inside and outside the church, hide pockets of their heart from God?

One reason: it feels safer. We insulate ourselves from pain when we love God with only a part of ourselves — or we think we do. If we don't put all our trust in God — if we don't love him with our whole selves — then if we think he's let us down, at least we have a backup plan. We still have ourselves to rely on. So we throw a few dollars in God's direction or attend a religious service or two. But deep inside, we're deathly afraid. We try to satisfy God with our works and honor him with our lips. But when it comes down to it, we don't feel safe opening our hearts to a God who killed his own Son. We'd rather have a God we can manage and control.

King David could relate. One day he was in the middle of worshiping God. He summoned thirty thousand Israelites to join him in transporting the ark of God. The Bible, in 2 Samuel 6:1 – 10, says, "They set the ark of God on a new cart and brought it from the house of Abinadab, which was on the hill." All was well; they were praising God. "David and the whole house of Israel were celebrating with all their might before the LORD, with songs and with harps, lyres, tambourines, sistrums and cymbals."

The next minute everything changed. "When they came to the threshing floor of Nacon, Uzzah reached out and took hold of the ark of God, because the oxen stumbled. The LORD's anger burned against

Uzzah because of his irreverent act; therefore God struck him down and he died there beside the ark of God."

God killed Uzzah on the spot—talk about shutting down a worship service! The mood changed. Notice David's reaction. "David was afraid of the Lord that day and said, 'How can the ark of the Lord ever come to me?'" His fear consumed him. Rather than continuing with the transportation of the ark, he stopped everything. "He was not willing to take the ark of the Lord to be with him in the City of David. Instead, he took it aside to the house of Obed-Edom the Gittite" (2 Samuel 6:1–10).

Three months went by. This is how long David waited. This is how long the ark sat still, and maybe David's relationship with God did too. The Scriptures are silent on this point.

But something finally changed. Eventually David picked up the whole transportation process again. "So David went down and brought up the ark of God from the house of Obed-Edom to the City of David with rejoicing." This time he approached the process with a little more intensity and focus. After they had taken six steps, he felt the need to turn his attention to the Lord. The Bible says, "When those who were carrying the ark of the Lord had taken six steps, he sacrificed a bull and a fattened calf." David wanted to be intimately involved in the process. He wanted to express his interconnected love for the Lord, and so he did. "David, wearing a linen ephod, danced before the Lord with all his might" (2 Samuel 6:12–14).

David found the secret to transcending his fear of God, but it didn't happen overnight. David was truly afraid when God killed Uzzah, and it seemed like his relationship with God took on a different flavor for a period of time. He retreated for a season, but the Bible tells us that what drew David back was God's goodness.

Although Obed-Edom wasn't even an Israelite, the ark of God stayed at his house for those three months. He was just a random guy. Isn't that like God, blessing us even when we don't deserve it?

We're not even told if Obed-Edom was a follower of God. But God blessed him all the same. "The ark of the LORD remained in the house of Obed-Edom the Gittite for three months, and the LORD blessed him and his entire household" (2 Samuel 6:11).

Evidently, God's blessing was so significant that it made the evening news. People noticed. "Now King David was told, 'The LORD has blessed the household of Obed-Edom and everything he has, because of the ark of God'" (2 Samuel 6:12). Why would this news motivate David to resume the transportation of the ark back to his own house? Maybe he needed to be reminded that God was good. He certainly knew God wasn't safe—Uzzah's death proved that. But David knew he could trust God because God is good.

The Bible teaches that God's grace melts our hearts: "God's kindness leads you toward repentance" (Romans 2:4). Grace changed David's mind and grace allowed him to resume an interconnected love for God. Grace even caused him to "dance before the LORD with all his might."

Safer Isn't Better

We might as well accept it. God is unsafe—no wonder we prefer a disconnected love with him. But unsafe sounds scary only until we also acknowledge that God is good. David remembered this, and if we want to be relevant, we too must remember this.

In *The Lion, the Witch and the Wardrobe*, C. S. Lewis highlights this comforting truth. The children are about to meet Aslan, and through their conversation with Mr. and Mrs. Beaver, it's obvious they're apprehensive about a personal encounter with the king.

"Is he—a man?" asked Lucy.

"Aslan a man!" said Mr. Beaver sternly. "Certainly not. I tell you he is the King of the wood and son of the great Emperor-

Beyond-the-Sea. Don't you know who is the King of the Beasts? Aslan is a lion — *the* lion, the great Lion."

"Ooh!" said Susan, "I'd thought he was a man. Is he — quite safe? I shall feel rather nervous about meeting a lion."

"That you will, dearie, and no mistake," said Mrs. Beaver, "if there's anyone who can appear before Aslan without their knees knocking, they're either braver than most or else just silly."

"Then he isn't safe?" said Lucy.

"Safe?" said Mr. Beaver; "don't you hear what Mrs. Beaver tells you? Who said anything about safe? 'Course he isn't safe. But he's good. He's the King I tell you."

If we're honest, we're all nervous about an interconnected love relationship with God. So most of us turn the radio up and turn our prayers down. We work longer. We bury ourselves in our kids, our hobbies, the stock market, or anything else that can drown out the nagging voice that there's something more to our relationship with God than polite behavior on Sunday mornings.

We give God our leftovers. We give him everything except ourselves. Like good Separatists, we labor a lifetime to lay good works at his feet, when what he wanted all along was us.

Others of us have given up on the whole "good works" scene. We think we're wicked, so we live it up. We figure it's not worth the effort to please a God who's never pleased. So we merely exist for ourselves. Like good Conformists, we're content with our discontentment and numb the ache with food, achievements, and the latest television show.

Whatever camp we lean toward, we fail to love God with our whole selves. Instead, we're only a shell and a shadow of what we're intended to be. In an effort to self-preserve and self-protect, we love God only partially and so harm ourselves.

The true God wants more. He wants all of us.

God tells us that a disconnected love is an imperfect love. The apostle John wrote,

> There is no fear in love. But perfect love drives out fear, because fear has to do with punishment. The one who fears is not made perfect in love.
>
> 1 John 4:18

Loving God connectedly is difficult because it means we'll lose control—or at least our perception of control. This type of love leads us through uncharted waters and along unexamined paths. Although unsafe, that's what makes it so exciting. Within this context God shows up in a remarkable way because then we actually need him. And when God is present in this way, then we naturally embody relevance because God embodies us just as Jesus promised:

> Anyone who loves me will be loved by my Father, and I too will love them and show myself to them.
>
> John 14:21 TNIV

Step Two

In the beginning of the chapter we examined how relevance is possible only when we have an interconnected love relationship with God. That was the easier of the two steps.

Once we have a love for God, what's the secret to growing that love? It is this: Our love for God grows only as our *need* for him grows.

We've already seen how people like the Pharisees didn't love God much because they didn't feel they needed God much. They thought they were pretty good already. Only the people who realize they *need* God actually *love* God. Luke, in chapter 7, illustrates this in a story about Jesus, a prostitute, and a Pharisee.

A Pharisee invited Jesus over to his house for dinner. Everything was going fine until *she* showed up.

When a woman who had lived a sinful life in that town learned that Jesus was eating at the Pharisee's house, she brought an alabaster jar of perfume, and as she stood behind him at his feet weeping, she began to wet his feet with her tears. Then she wiped them with her hair, kissed them and poured perfume on them.

The Pharisee, named Simon, knew exactly who she was. It's likely the whole town did—after all, she did have a reputation. Even though Simon was judgmental, he didn't want to blow his cover.

When the Pharisee who had invited him saw this, he said to himself, "If this man were a prophet, he would know who is touching him and what kind of woman she is—that she is a sinner."

Because he was the Son of God, Jesus knew what Simon was thinking. "Simon, I have something to tell you."

Simon responded, "Tell me, teacher."

"Two men owed money to a certain moneylender," Jesus said. "One owed him five hundred denarii, and the other fifty. Neither of them had the money to pay him back, so he canceled the debts of both. Now which of them will love him more?"

Simon thought about it and said, "I suppose the one who had the bigger debt canceled."

"You have judged correctly," Jesus said.

Then he asked Simon, "Do you see this woman? I came into your house. You did not give me any water for my feet, but she wet my feet with her tears and wiped them with her hair. You did not give me a kiss, but this woman, from the time I entered, has not stopped kissing my feet. You did not put oil on my head, but she has poured perfume on my feet. Therefore, I tell you, her many sins have been forgiven—for she loved much. But he who has been forgiven little loves little" (Luke 7:37–47).

Jesus said the size of our love for God is directly proportionate to the level of our need for his forgiveness. The key isn't how *much* we

sin, but rather how *much we know* that we sin. The diagram below
may help.

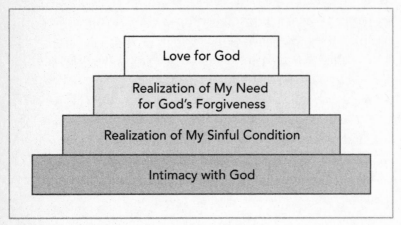

Figure 9.1: Depth of Love Diagram

The secret to increasing our love for God is to increase our need
for God. The problem is that most of us never sense our need for God
because we hang out with other humans too much. We start comparing ourselves to others, and then we think we're pretty hot stuff.

Only we're not supposed to compare ourselves to other people.
That's what the Pharisees did. They convinced themselves that God
was lucky to have them on his team. They put on a great performance and showed everyone else up. Pride slowly crept in, but so did
ingratitude. And ingratitude sucks away our need for God and thus
our love for God. Who needs God if you're already perfect?

We only realize the depth of our sinfulness when we're in the
presence of someone free from sin—God himself. And this is exactly
what the woman in Luke's gospel did. She got into God's presence
—she even knelt at his feet. When we're intimate with God, we see
ourselves for who we truly are, and we see him for who he truly is.
Then there's nothing we can do but throw ourselves upon his mercy.

What happens next?

God forgives us.

And then our love for him grows exponentially. Jesus told Simon that those who have been forgiven much love much.

The prophet Isaiah knew this. For all we know, Isaiah was a pretty righteous guy — after all, he *was* a prophet. But examine this encounter Isaiah had with God:

> I saw the Lord seated on a throne, high and exalted, and the train of his robe filled the temple. Above him were seraphs, each with six wings: With two wings they covered their faces, with two they covered their feet, and with two they were flying. And they were calling to one another: "Holy, holy, holy is the LORD Almighty; the whole earth is full of his glory." At the sound of their voices the doorposts and thresholds shook and the temple was filled with smoke. "Woe to me!" I cried. "I am ruined! For I am a man of unclean lips, and I live among a people of unclean lips, and my eyes have seen the King, the LORD Almighty."
>
> Isaiah 6:1–5

Isaiah was undone when he saw God in all his glory. As Isaiah's intimacy with God increased, the realization of his sinfulness increased, which in turn caused him to have a greater need for God's forgiveness. He saw himself as a man in desperate need of God's mercy and grace. This process propelled him to have a greater love for God.

When we see ourselves as self-sufficient, then our love for God is small. We aren't grateful because, in our minds, there's no need for grace. On the other hand, when we acknowledge our sinfulness, which happens only as we enter God's presence, then we understand our need for him. This is the melody line throughout the entire Bible: "God opposes the proud but gives grace to the humble" (James 4:6).

Jesus hit these same notes in the Beatitudes. He said, "Blessed are the poor in spirit, for theirs is the kingdom of heaven" (Matthew 5:3). This term "poor in spirit" actually means spiritually bankrupt. This Greek word *ptochos* refers to someone who crouches and cowers in a beggarly fashion. Jesus said that the kingdom of heaven belongs to those who perceive themselves as spiritually desperate and bankrupt.

What's so significant about spiritual bankruptcy?

It's the only condition from which God can lift us up. It's uncomfortable, though, to consider ourselves in this image. We're used to viewing ourselves as upright and worthy, and it's to this self-image that we now turn our attention.

CHAPTER 10

POSITION
IS EVERYTHING

Andre Agassi, the now retired tennis phenom, used to have hair.

Some younger folk might not know this critical factoid, but we older people saw it with our own two eyes. Back in the eighties he rocked a flowing mullet, a fluorescent headband, and yellow Spandex underneath denim shorts. In the last decade, Agassi has been sporting a shaved head and baggy, plain-colored duds.

Let me assure you, I don't care. I only know these important truths because of commercials bought and paid for by Canon. Agassi, their celebrity endorser, concluded every commercial by staring at the viewer and declaring, "Image is everything." After twenty years I still remember their tagline.

Canon, however, got this statement only half right. I think the tagline should have been, "Position is everything." Position, after all, is a critical component in achieving life on the fine line.

In Love with Ourselves

Remember, relevance is possible only when we love God connectedly and when we love our neighbor as ourselves. The common problem for most of us isn't that we don't love our neighbor, but rather that we don't love ourselves the right way.

You might think the last thing we need to focus on is loving ourselves better. Isn't our society already completely self-consumed? Scottish preacher Alexander Whyte thought so. He wrote:

> It is out of self-love that all our other evil passions spring. The whole fall and ruin and misery of our present human nature lies in this, that in every human being self-love has taken, in addition to its own place, the place of the love of God and of the love of man also. We naturally now love nothing and no one but ourselves.[1]

Yet my strong belief is that we need to focus more of our energies on loving ourselves better—not *more*, but *better*.

Here's why. Although I can't speak for everyone, my experience tells me that the majority of us view ourselves the wrong way. Most of us act out of self-hatred, not self-love, whether believers or unbelievers. On the outside it looks like everything is fine, but a closer look reveals something different. We're cutters, drug users, and alcoholics; we're shopaholics, workaholics, and churchaholics. We suffer from anorexia, bulimia, and gluttony. We gossip, steal, and lead lives of secret sexual sin. And *we're* supposed to love our neighbors like we love ourselves?

This problem of loving ourselves the wrong way isn't unique to our generation. Church history doesn't paint a better picture. Throughout the centuries many believers didn't love themselves the right way either. They willingly inflicted physical pain upon themselves, ranging from extreme fasting to severing body parts. Asceticism was intended to earn God's love and forgiveness by communicating the sinner's extreme remorse to God. At first glance, asceticism sounds extremely pious, but a deeper look reveals something else. It is a dark corruption of proper self-love. When believers reenacted these forms of self-punishment as penance for sin, they communicated by their actions that Christ's payment on the cross wasn't sufficient payment for their sin.

The ascetics were self-centered, not other-centered. They were so fascinated with themselves that all they could think about was their own sinfulness. Focusing on others would have shifted their mind-set off themselves and off their weaknesses. Many ascetics suffered from pride because Christianity became a competition about who could endure the most suffering. Who gave them permission to stop when they were the ones initiating the pain? I don't know about you, but I don't want ascetics loving me the way they love themselves. It would be hazardous to my health.

Our generation isn't all that different. Not many of us whip ourselves, but we're just as self-consumed, and our self-love is just as twisted. The average person has multiple credit cards maxed to the limit. Rather than meditating upon spiritual things, our minds are constantly consumed with material things. We want the latest, the coolest, and the best. We're addicted to the earthly — and to the illusion that possessions will satisfy our souls.

If honest, many of us feel empty and unfulfilled. In our hearts we're idolaters and adulterers. Whether we're addicted to pain or pleasure, asceticism or hedonism, we'll never be relevant. Whether we're Separatists or Conformists, we fail to love ourselves the right way, the way God loves us. So when it comes time to love others as ourselves, we love others the wrong way too.

But it doesn't have to be this way.

Where Are You Seated?

We believers tend to live only in light of our condition, of *how* we are. We fail to live in light of our position, of *who* we are. Our condition is the way we behave, act, and think in a given moment. Our position is the standing, privilege, and status we have because of Christ.

Let me give you a practical illustration. My guess is that at this very moment, just like me, you're probably seated somewhere, perhaps on a plane or in a coffee shop. If you were to ask me where I'm seated, I would say in an office chair. If you asked where, I'd say in Columbus, Ohio. We could go on to say the United States, North America, and so on. These statements are true, but not complete. My answers all reflect an emphasis upon my condition. I failed to answer the question in light of my position. If I did, I would have said that I am also seated in the heavenly realms with Christ Jesus, which I could do based on Ephesians 2:6. I *am* here on earth, conditionally, but since I'm a follower of Christ, I'm *also* seated in heaven, positionally.

Some might see this just as semantics, but it's much more than that. Let's say a certain believer looks at pornography. The way his brain responds after he sins will tell us whether he's focused on his condition or his position.

If he's focused on his condition, he'll say things like, "Man, I'm such a loser. I'm a pervert. I'll never overcome this addiction. What would people think of me if they knew I did this? I'm a sick, self-centered idiot." These comments focus on *how* he is. Since he engaged in sinful conduct, he sees himself only for his sin. The Enemy has deceived him into living in only one dimension. His thoughts continually rehearse the following:

My Condition — How I Am ...	
Abusive to others	Gossiper
Betrayer of friends	Hateful
Crass in speech	Incompatible
Deceitful	Jealous of others
Enslaved to flesh	Keeper of grudges
Fake	Lustful in thoughts

Materialistic	Too fat
Never satisfied	Ugly
Overeater	Violent to my family
Perverted	Workaholic
Quitter	Xpistos (Christ's) enemy
Reluctant to do good	Yoked with sin
Sexually addicted	Zealous of strife

Figure 10.1: ABCs of My Condition

Contrast this with a person focused on his position. After sinning he'll say things like, "That wasn't the real me. I don't have to say yes to sin. In Christ I can overcome all things. I am more than the sin that wants to overtake me." This type of talk is focused on *who* he is. It's reflective of his standing, privilege, and status because of Christ. This person consciously recognizes that another dimension exists. His thoughts rehearse the following:

My Position — Who I Am ...

Accepted in the beloved	New creation
Bought with a price	One spirit with the Lord
Crucified with Christ	Perfect in Christ
Dwelt by the Holy Spirit	Quieted in who God is
Enslaved to God	Raised up with him
Freed from slavery to sin	Seated in heavenly places
God's child	Transformed into Christ's image
Heir of God's riches	United to the Lord
In him completeness	Victorious through my Lord
Jesus' chosen inheritance	Wonderfully made
Kingly priest	Xpistos (Christ's) workmanship
Light of the world	Yoked with righteousness
Mastered no longer by sin	Zealous of good work

Figure 10.2: ABCs of My Position

If you've trusted Jesus as your Lord and Savior, each of these positional statements is true about you, whether you feel like they are or not. You don't have to wait until you reach heaven for them to be true. They're not dependent upon feelings, time, behavior, or anything else. They're true simply because God said so, and God doesn't lie (Titus 1:2).

Once we've become a follower of Jesus, God no longer views us as anything less than perfect. When he sees us, he sees the righteousness of Christ. We're fully accepted and we don't have to perform in order to stay on his good side. The Bible says that once we've truly been saved, nothing we do can separate us from the love of God, and he'll never love us any more or any less than he already does (Romans 8:39).

These two realities, condition and position, are in direct opposition to one another. They have everything to do with how God views us and how we view ourselves. Notice how the Bible compares and contrasts them:

Condition		Position	
How I Am	Rom. 7:19–21	Who I Am	Eph. 1:4, 18
Old Person	Gal. 5:24; Rom. 6:6	New Person	Rom. 6:4, 22
Temporal	2 Cor. 4:18	Eternal	2 Cor. 4:18
Seen	2 Cor. 4:18	Unseen	2 Cor. 4:18
Physical	Rom. 7:18	Spiritual	1 Cor. 1:2
False Self	Rom. 7:17	True Self	2 Cor. 5:17

Figure 10.3: Condition vs. Position

Like most of us today, the believers in first-century Ephesus were too focused on their *condition*. The apostle Paul, knowing their poverty of understanding, begins his letter to the Ephesians with a prayer. He begs God to let them understand their *position*.

He writes, "I pray also that the eyes of your heart may be enlightened in order that you may know the hope to which he has called you, the riches of his glorious inheritance in the saints, and his incomparably great power for us who believe" (Ephesians 1:18–19).

Then Paul does something extremely practical. He tells them exactly who they are in Christ. The book of Ephesians details the spiritual wealth already available to them because of Jesus. All that Christ attained has been credited to their accounts. Paul spends the first three chapters of Ephesians telling the believers *who they are*. There is only one imperative in this entire section. He wants to let the reality of their position sink in. But in the last three chapters he tells them *how they should be*. There are forty imperatives in this section.

His logic is obvious: We can't live like we're supposed to until we first know who we are. We must first understand our position before we can apply it to our condition. Most of us—and most of our churches—have it backwards. We focus on how we should live without ever knowing who we really are. We strap a burden of duty to our backs without understanding the power by which we're supposed to carry it. And so most of us face life in the power of our flesh, never recognizing that Jesus desires to carry our burdens for us.

But we were never meant to live life in our own strength. We need to take a different approach and follow Paul's example—to fill our heads and hearts with the reality of who we are in Christ. We need to understand the power of our position. Only then will we be able to become *how* we were born to be.

When the Cat's Away

I loved sixth grade, mostly because of Miss Bristol. She read us books like *The Tower of Geburah* while we sat on carpet squares. She had something called the "warm fuzzy" jar that was filled with candy, and she let us choose a sweet reward if she caught us being good.

One day Miss Bristol didn't show up, and she ended up being sick for the entire week. We had a substitute teacher, and my typically wonderful behavior slowly began to slip. Basically, I acted like a punk. I wrote notes, talked out of turn, and showed little respect to our substitute.

Toward the end of the week, my friend Luke decided to shake things up. After lunch, Luke snuck a roll of toilet paper back to his seat. When the substitute turned to write on the chalkboard, Luke threw the roll across the room in my direction. It trailed a perfect paper tail behind. The class giggled, of course, but by the time the substitute turned around, there was nothing to see. Luke motioned for me to throw the roll back to him. I held the roll behind my head like a quarterback holding a football and, with as much power as a sixth grader could muster, I released the roll.

In slow motion, the white paper trail began to form, like a space shuttle in flight. A blaze of glory unfurled in the air—but too slowly! By the time the roll reached its zenith, the substitute had already turned around to face the class. All the noise was immediately sucked out of the room as if by a vortex. The entire class sat transfixed in silence, mouths gaping, wondering what would happen next.

Nonchalantly, the substitute walked to her desk and referenced the seating chart. "Kary," she barked, "I'm writing your name in the book. Miss Bristol is going to get a description of your bad behavior, and she can deal with you."

Fear immediately flowed through my veins. If only she would send me straight to the principal—at least then I wouldn't have to face Miss Bristol.

The weekend crawled by and Monday finally came. Miss Bristol returned and, sure enough, she called me out of class and into the hallway. She looked me right in the eyes and said, "Kary, you're one of my right-hand men. I look up to you."

I waited for more. I wanted more—for her to hit me over the

head with a hammer or something. At a minimum she could have yelled and told me how bad I was. That would have confirmed how I felt inside.

But her strategy was different. Instead of focusing on my condition — *how* I was — she focused on my position — *who* I was. And boy, was it effective. The rest of the year my behavior flowed from my position. I acted like one of her right-hand men because that's how she addressed me. The way Miss Bristol viewed me changed how I viewed myself.

Paul's Prerogative

Miss Bristol must have gotten her strategy from the apostle Paul because the church of Corinth received a similar bad report — minus the roll of toilet paper.

Paul stepped away from this church for a period of time. Rather than behaving, the Corinthian Christians earned quite a reputation for misbehaving. They were known as one of the most sinful churches in the New Testament, getting into fights over who baptized who, paying more attention to their ministers than to Jesus (1 Corinthians 1:11 – 12). They even were arrogant about a gross sexual sin that took place in their community (1 Corinthians 5:1 – 2). A certain man was sleeping with his stepmother. Rather than grieving this behavior, they bragged about it while they shopped for groceries. Their experience with the Lord's Supper wasn't any better (1 Corinthians 11:20 – 21, 28 – 30). When they gathered for communion, a few went away starving while others stuffed their faces — and even got drunk on the communion wine!

God was so grieved that he took some of their lives in judgment. To say the Corinthians' condition was sinful is an understatement. Word got back to Paul, and, of course, he fired off a letter.

Now imagine you're Paul. Imagine you've invested your sweat, blood, and tears in establishing this church. You laid your life on the line for them. How would you feel about this bad report? How would you start your letter to them? Perhaps "To the scum at Corinth" or maybe "Dear clueless Corinthians." But this isn't what Paul did. He didn't begin by addressing their condition, but rather their position. He wrote, "To the church of God which is at Corinth, to those who have been sanctified in Christ Jesus, saints by calling" (1 Corinthians 1:2 NASB). Paul addressed these *saints* in light of *who* they were and not *how* they were. And it made all the difference.

In reading Paul's second letter to the Corinthians, we can see that his little lesson on position must have hit the target. These Christians turned the corner, and although not perfect, they started to let *who* they were seep into *how* they were, and it transformed the face of their church. At the point when Paul penned his first letter to the Corinthians, these Christians carried with them a casual approach to sin. Yet by his next letter they transitioned to judging sin with grace and compassion (2 Corinthians 2). And although previously we caught them selfishly gorging their faces at communion, in this second letter we now see them selflessly collecting resources for the needs of other churches around them (2 Corinthians 8–9).

In this entire conversation, of course, we're not just turning a blind eye to our condition. Although Paul started out in the first chapter by reminding the Corinthians of who they were, a couple chapters later he also reminded them about how they were. He disapproved of their sinful conduct and called them to a higher standard, one of moral purity. But this was only after he strengthened them with the power of their position. His pattern was to empower first, exhort second.

We too must first recognize who we are in Christ before we can ever attempt to live righteously in this life. As we maintain an intimate relationship with the Lord, we not only learn more about our position but also more about our condition. We not only understand *his* blessings but also *our* bankruptcy. As we come to learn more of Jesus' strengths, we naturally come to learn more of our weaknesses.

We can see this in Paul's life. The more clearly Paul saw his Savior, the more clearly he saw his sin. He reflected this in his letters. Earlier in his life he referred to himself as the least of the apostles—a humble statement, yes, but one that leaves room for improvement (1 Corinthians 15:9). But as time went on, he understood more of his capacity to sin. He classified himself as the least of all the saints (Ephesians 3:8). Finally, after tasting a lifetime of his own sinful tendencies, he gave himself a new title—the chief of sinners (1 Timothy 1:15). The more he understood *God's* potential in him, the more he understood *his own* potential to sin. This instilled humility and dependence because he knew that unless God empowered him to live a holy life, he was hopeless. Reflecting on this he wrote, "I know that nothing good lives in me, that is, in my sinful nature. For I have the desire to do what is good, but I cannot carry it out" (Romans 7:18).

The Power of Position

No one can argue with the fact that Jesus was relevant to everyone he met. But how? How did the Son of God find it in himself to take on the position of a servant and come to the earth to give his life for you and for me?

The Scriptures are clear: Jesus' service flowed out of his understanding of his position.

I often ask Christians, "Besides Jesus' death on the cross, what act best depicted his love and servanthood for others?"

Nine times out of ten when I ask this question, I get the same answer: when he washed the disciples' feet.

Why is this act so poignant in our minds? It's been the focus of many sermons and books. Even the business world has latched on to this event, citing it in the recent surge of books and articles on servant-leadership.

A peek into first-century culture helps a bit. Washing feet was the work of a slave, and the twelve disciples were in a tight race to prove who was the greatest—who would have the prominent position in the kingdom (Matthew 20:20–28). But Jesus tied a towel around his waist, filled a basin with water, and knelt to wash his disciples' dirty, calloused feet. Jesus, ever the relevant servant, took the job upon himself.

In this story most of us focus on the act of washing the disciples' feet. This tends to be the main emphasis. But even though the act itself was significant, something else was even more noteworthy. We rarely notice Jesus' thought process before he picked up the towel. John tells us that "Jesus knew that the Father had put all things under his power, and that he had come from God and was returning to God; so he got up from the meal" and "began to wash his disciples' feet" (John 13:3–5).

What liberated Jesus to serve others in this relevant way? His position.

Not guilt. Not a sense of duty or desire to perform. All he did was remind himself of who he was. He knew his position was secure with the Father and that he didn't have to prove anything, so he was able to love and serve others. He was able to meet the needs of everyone in the room. While the disciples were paralyzed with the need to *prove* their position, Jesus *rested* in his.

Our position as children of the Most High God liberates us to love others. We step outside the posturing game when we acknowledge that our position is already secure. When we view ourselves the right way, the way God does, we'll stop seeing others as a threat. And when we love ourselves the right way, the way God does, we can love others the right way too. The fine line is closer than we think.

PART IV

HOW DO WE DO IT?

*Think like a wise man but communicate
in the language of the people.*
William Butler Yeats

CHAPTER 11

PERFECT
BLUE BUILDINGS

"You two should really meet. I know you'll like the way each other thinks."

After hearing that comment for about the fifth time, I took it as a sign from God that he wanted me to meet John McCollum. And so it was that I found myself driving to meet John at his design firm, Element, in Clintonville, Ohio, a Columbus neighborhood just north of the Ohio State University campus.

When I pulled up, I was expecting at the least "unconventional" and at the most "eccentric," but nothing could have prepared me for the entire front door painted Smurf blue.

Things soon got even stranger. At the top of the narrow staircase, I noticed some odd photographs: they were all pictures of Asian children who were obviously poor but, equally clearly, were hopeful. I began to wonder if I'd wandered into the wrong door, and the green, orange, and purple walls didn't convince me otherwise. Was this a design firm or an international daycare?

Later I learned that John moved into the building in 1999, though at the time it lacked its colorful flare. In fact, the first time John visited the property, all the windows were boarded up, and it looked like a crack house. It took John some time to track down the landlord and some more time to convince the landlord to agree to lease such a filthy abandoned place. But John saw something and he proved it on the spot by signing a five-year lease.

Tattoos Tell Stories

On this day, there was no trace of the building's former condition. The man behind that amazing transition sat behind his computer, dressed in the designer de rigueur of T-shirt and jeans. "Hey, Kary," John said, and a charismatic smile beamed up at me.

I reciprocated and, as an afterthought, commented on the colorful tattoo—from what I could see greens, whites, and grays—only partially covered by his sleeve. Treating my compliment as an open door, John went on to enthusiastically describe the inspiration behind his ink. Proudly John pulled up his sleeve, and then it happened.

Up until that moment my brain had been firing on one cylinder, but when I gazed upon the tattoo, now exposed in its fullness, I had several competing thoughts all at once. John's tattoo wasn't the typical tribal band but, rather, a twisted paradox of innocence and evil, beauty and ugliness.

Covering his entire right shoulder in painstaking detail, four distinct images told one single story—only this story was richly laced with emotion. I first noticed the white dove, head pointed down, abnormally peaceful.

But as quick as tranquility entered my mind, it was swallowed up —literally. Wrapping itself seductively around this serene bird was a yellow-green snake, forked tongue and all. The snake looked curiously wise, like it knew something I didn't.

Strategically interwoven around these two creatures, a padlock connected heavy chain links. Affixed to one of the chain links hung a worn-looking price tag, bearing the number "1." And almost as an afterthought my brain caught two words — *Engage* and *Unleash* — scripted in cursive.

The tattoo, he told me, was inspired by a photograph of a boy that haunted him. He saw it years earlier at the Toul Sleng Genocide Museum in Phnom Penh, the capital of Cambodia. The museum is built on the site of the notorious Security Prison 21 that was operated by the Khmer Rouge regime in the late 1970s. The buildings at Toul Sleng, meaning "Hill of the Poisonous Trees," were once enclosed in electrified barbed wire and honeycombed with prison cells. Countless Cambodians were imprisoned, tortured, and killed in Security Prison 21, and the buildings and fittings, including residual bloodstains, have been preserved intact as evidence against the regime.

John went on. Upon arrival, prisoners were photographed, interrogated, stripped, and taken to their cells, where they were shackled to the walls, the concrete floor, or long pieces of iron bar along with other prisoners. They slept on the floor without mats, mosquito nets, or blankets. As John told the story, his voice cracked several times.

"When I close my eyes, I can see the photograph clearly. I can see his face. He didn't have a name, only a number '1' pinned to his shirt. So I call him Boy Number 1. The saddest thing," John continued, "is that he had heavy chains around his neck.

"He was around eight or nine — not much older than my sons. A large padlock kept the chain around his neck in place. The photograph affected me so much that I knew someday I needed to have chains and a padlock tattooed someplace on my body."

Intrigued, I attempted to put together the missing pieces. "But what about the serpent, the dove, and the words — "

"The serpent and the dove are because of my tattoo artist," John said, cutting me off. His tattoo artist wanted to know the story behind the chains before she inked him. John told her about Boy Number 1. He also told her about Jesus' words to his followers, in the gospel of Matthew (10:16), before he sent them out. "I am sending you out like sheep among wolves. Therefore be as shrewd as snakes and as innocent as doves."

"Although unfamiliar with the Gospels, my tattoo artist liked Jesus' words," John explained. "So she asked me if she could draft an idea that incorporated that imagery."

"Thus, the serpent and the dove," I filled in.

"Right on," John responded. "And these words *Engage* and *Unleash* complete the tattoo. They're short for *Engage Suffering* and *Unleash Hope.* My wife, Kori, and I have adopted that as our family's mission statement. It's also the unofficial motto for our orphanages in Asia."

"Orphanages in Asia?" I asked. "I thought you owned a design firm."

"I do. But I also cofounded an organization called Asia's Hope. It's a long story. Tell you what, let's grab lunch and I'll start from the beginning."

We headed downstairs, my head and heart spinning as we left the rainbow walls of Element and headed toward a nearby deli.

An Unusual Lunch

Picking up where we left off, John continued the dialogue. I shut up, savored my mushroom and mozzarella wrap, and gave my full attention to the story unfolding before me. John told me about 1998, a significant year for him and Kori for a couple of reasons. Even though to their knowledge they were able to have children, they decided to pursue international adoption. They were matched with a Vietnamese boy named Chien, and in July of that year they flew overseas to meet him and bring him home.

After getting off the plane in Vietnam, John was staggered by the poverty. He saw moms begging for food and homeless kids thronging the streets. In that moment, he and Kori committed their future to God as missionaries in Vietnam if the Lord chose to lead them in that way. After three weeks spent climbing mountains of paperwork, John and Kori boarded a plane back to America with their new son, Chien.

This wasn't the only change in their lives that year—John left his secure job at an ad agency and started Element. "Sounds like 1998 was a year of faith for you and Kori," I observed.

"It gets more interesting," he said.

Later that year, John and Kori were having dinner with Rebecca and her husband, friends of theirs from church. That evening Rebecca told them about a young Korean woman who was trying to find a family to adopt her unborn child. Knowing that John and Kori were familiar with the whole process, having recently adopted Chien, Rebecca asked them to pray for this woman, her child, and their situation. Evidently, no families were coming forward to adopt the child.

Soon after that, John couldn't sleep one night. He woke Kori. "This may sound strange, but do you think that we're supposed to adopt that baby?"

Miraculously, God had been working in Kori's heart. "I didn't want to say anything to you because I didn't want to pressure you."

So with Chien's adoption finalized only a few months earlier, they initiated the process to adopt the new baby they would name Pak.

"That's a crazy story, John," I said, without even thinking.

"I'll tell you what's crazy," he said, leaning forward. "We only found this out after the fact, but Pak's birth mom was confident we were going to be the adoptive family."

"What do you mean?"

"Before Pak's birth, his mom had confided in Rebecca's mother, Hazel, that she was afraid she wouldn't find an American family who would love and adopt her Asian child. Hazel had tried to console her, telling her that friends of her daughter had just adopted a boy named Chien from Vietnam."

Evidently those words stuck with Pak's birth mom because after a few days, before John and Kori even knew that Pak existed, his birth mom confidently told Hazel, "I prayed about it. The family that adopted the boy from Vietnam is supposed to adopt my baby too."

Cambodian Beer

"Hey, where did you get that shirt?" John shouted to a confused stranger across the room. "Angkor Beer," John said. "That's the national beer of Cambodia."

The young man smiled, glad someone appreciated his cool shirt, and walked over.

"I work with orphanages in Cambodia and Thailand," John explained. "In fact, I just got back from a trip visiting all my kids."

"Really." The young man sounded genuinely interested. "I was in Cambodia with my church this past summer on a mission trip. That's where I got this shirt."

Though strangers only moments before, these two world travelers were bonding right before my eyes. I, on the other hand, just stood there feeling out of place.

After lunch John and I continued our conversation back in his office. "Are you sure you want to hear more?" John asked.

"Are you kidding? Keep it coming. This story is amazing. Tell me about Asia's Hope," I suggested, attempting to steer the conversation.

"Oh, yeah. I'm getting close to that. After Pak's adoption we were living off credit cards in order to pay my new Element employees. Element was a little unorthodox from the beginning. We didn't really look or function like a traditional design firm."

"Really," I said sarcastically. "The Smurf blue door told me otherwise."

John laughed. "Well, we *were* kind of making things up as we went along."

John's unconventional approach to running a business occasionally frustrated his employees. He had a habit of inviting people over to talk about God or orphans in Asia. These one-on-one meetings soon evolved into more. John opened up his office space in order to host occasional community events. Oddly, John viewed Element as a venue in which to serve people and meet their needs.

He juggled this delicate balance of work, play, and ministry. But it was more than a juggling act. Rather than compartmentalizing these core areas of his life (work, play, ministry), he intentionally integrated them — something all Transformists do. This blending of life is captured in one of my favorite quotes by François-René de Chateaubriand:

> A master in the art of living draws no sharp distinction between his work and his play; his labor and his leisure; his mind and his body; his education and his recreation. He hardly knows which is which. He simply pursues his vision of excellence through whatever he is doing, and leaves others to determine whether he is working or playing. To himself, he always appears to be doing both.[1]

About the only thing that wasn't blended into the McCollums' lives was the location of the church they attended. Although Element was in Clintonville, their large suburban church wasn't. But even though they felt a clear call to leave, they didn't have another church to join, so they stayed another three and a half years. They didn't just want to leave a ministry; they wanted to be sent to another. So they made the most of their time. Periodically John preached and led worship for the young adult service, while Kori helped lead the children. Still, during quiet moments they felt a strong leading that God had more in store for them.

Coffee Break

"You want some coffee?" asked John. "Follow me."

Walking into a makeshift kitchen for the employees, John grabbed a mug and informed me proudly that he roasted his own coffee beans. While I relied on the professionals at Caribou to handle my coffee needs, I took a chance on John's roasting skills, and I was rewarded with the best cup of coffee I'd ever tasted. As we headed back to John's office, I asked again about the orphanage.

We sat down and John finally told me the story. "At the time we adopted Chien and Pak we were working with the youth group. After a couple years of hearing Kori and me talk about the possibility of ministering in Vietnam, the youth pastor said, 'You always talk about Vietnam. Would you ever be willing to go to Cambodia? Because there's this pastor in Wooster who goes to Cambodia every year. Here's his number if you're interested.'"

John called the pastor, Dave Atkins, and two weeks later they were on a plane to Cambodia. When they landed, John said he immediately felt like he was home, but he was heartbroken. He saw a war-torn country, ravaged by poverty and prostitution. He saw beggars and orphans on nearly every street corner.

The average person visiting these parts of Cambodia wouldn't see much potential for this dirty, abandoned place, just like John's landlord didn't see much potential for his place in Clintonville. But John saw something more.

He was blown away by the generosity of the Cambodian Christians. Cambodian pastors make around four hundred dollars in a year, but they still gave to others who needed help. This made John feel guilty. Dave and he had digital cameras, MP3 players, and computers with them. The combined value of these items could be sold and used to feed several families for an entire year.

One day John said, "Dave, what are we going to do to take this to the next level?"

"What do you mean? We both work full-time jobs," Dave responded. "I feel like I'm doing as much as I can."

"It just seems like we have so much money compared to these Cambodians. Our problem is that we don't have a good knowledge of the culture or language. These Cambodians understand the culture and the language, but they have hardly any money."

Put like that, things seemed pretty clear. Something had to be done. John gave Kori a call and tried to convey his deep feelings by phone. She knew they'd have a lot to talk about when he got back.

A few weeks later, John and Dave met halfway between Wooster and Clintonville, and over greasy diner food, on the back of paper napkins, they crafted a vision, a mission, core values, and a budget for Asia's Hope.

One of the first steps was to create a nonprofit and form a board. In those early months they funded the ministry through donations from friends, family members, and mission trip alumni. When they couldn't meet budget, they passed the hat at board meetings.

John and Dave clarified several project goals for Asia's Hope. The first was to start a university student center. They rented a building for poor Cambodian Christian college kids. Less than 1 percent of Cambodian college students are Christians, and, without a strong support system, many of these students will flounder in their faith. The university student center helps them remain grounded by giving them room and board, leadership training, and practical ministry experience.

The second goal they identified was to build orphanages. These places give kids food, shelter, education, and a loving environment. Even more important, they help steer kids away from poverty and prostitution. Asia's Hope currently offers over two hundred kids a better chance at life.

Their third goal was to build a Christian school. This school exists primarily to provide a high-quality education for the children residing in their orphanages in and around Phnom Penh. The school, which currently offers kindergarten through fifth grade classes, is a member of the Association of Christian Schools International.

A Church Inside Element

"Sorry to interrupt, John"—a young man popped his head into the office—"I'll be using the office to do some counseling. Is that cool?"

"Yeah, Jeff, no problem," John said.

"Who's that?" I asked.

"Oh, that's Jeff Cannell. He's my pastor. He's using some office space at Element until my church, Central Vineyard, can get a building."

"So now you have counseling sessions going on right outside your door?"

"Yep. I'll tell you what, Kary, my church is amazing. It's made up of artists, intellectuals, and homeless people, as well as individuals recovering from alcoholism, drug addiction, and fundamentalism. We meet on Sundays right down the street from here in Clintonville."

"Since when did you switch churches?"

"Oh, yeah." John chuckled. "I guess I left you in the dark as to how it all ends. Well, one day Jeff, the guy you just met, stopped by. He's a buddy of mine from high school, and he told me that he was leaving his job as a suburban pastor. He and his wife, Adrienne, felt God leading them to start a church near their home in Clintonville. Jeff had a nice, comfortable job at a different suburban church than mine. He loved and respected his senior pastor and got some real good mentoring from him. But still, he couldn't shake it. God called them to leave and they were going to follow."

"I'm sensing a pattern here," I said. "God speaks, people obey."

"Kori and I knew this was the church we'd been waiting for. This was the ministry that we should be sent to. The beautiful thing was that our decision was supported by the leadership at our current church as well."

"They weren't scared of losing you guys? You both were leading some pretty viable ministries."

"Well, we were phasing out over time and replacing ourselves," John said. "But no, they weren't scared. They even invited Jeff to come to our last service and speak. Then they laid hands on us and sent us out to our new ministry."

"That's so cool, man. You know, being a pastor I rarely ever see it like that. Instead, it seems like people usually just leave overnight, like they don't care about leaving. Or other times the sending church doesn't want to let people go, so they don't really support them when they leave."

"No, it's been great," John said. "Now it seems like all areas of my life are integrated. In fact, a couple weeks ago, Jeff opened the door for me to share about Asia's Hope during a Sunday morning service."

"How did that happen?"

"Well, one day we were here in my office, and I was telling him about how difficult it was for a grassroots, volunteer-based organization to communicate with thousands of individual supporters. Our administration is a little overworked at the moment. Then Jeff said, 'Wouldn't it be cool if you could save some of that administrative headache by having one church sponsor an entire orphanage?'"

"That *would* be cool," I said. "A little unlikely, but still cool."

"That's what I thought," John said. "But then Jeff suggested, 'Let's have our church do it.' I told him it might be a bit expensive, seeing that we were a fairly new church. We only had a hundred and fifty people or so. But sure enough, Jeff invited me to share the vision of Asia's Hope on a Sunday morning."

"How did everyone respond?" I asked.

"I had mono that morning, so they had to kind of prop me up on stage," John recounted. "But I prayed, showed slides, cried a bit ... and then other people cried, and then I guess God moved in a strong way because enough money was pledged."

"How much money are we talking?"

"Well, it's about six thousand dollars in start-up costs. And then after that it's about two thousand a month."

"The price to change a kid's future."

"Thirty kids' futures," John reminded me.

Bigger Than a Building

That's what Transformists do. They shape the future by changing the present. They transform the world around them.

I ended up visiting John at his blue-door building more than a few times. Sometimes I was alone. Other times I brought a group of teens from my church. I had John tell the teens about Asia's Hope, and then we'd hit the streets and wash cars, donating all the proceeds to the orphanages. One kid named Luke couldn't believe that a single afternoon away from Xbox would keep a Cambodian orphan off the street for an entire year.

John opened my heart to experience God's heart for the poor in a way I'd never known. Of course, I knew it from the Scriptures. There are so many verses about God's compassion for the poor, the orphaned, and the widowed, but for some reason those words never sank in. That's all changed now. And it seems to be changing for a whole bunch of other people who follow Jesus too.

John told me that when he was young his parents wanted to adopt a girl from Asia, but it was too expensive. After seeing John and Kori obey God by adopting Chien and Pak, John's parents decided it was time to obey God, and in their fifties they adopted Sarah. Now John is blessed to have a sister from China, a dream he had given up in third grade.

I guess John and Kori were jealous because they adopted a little girl of their own. In 2006, they received Xiudan from China. Now they have three kids, each from a different country in Asia. And their hope, only found within Jesus Christ, continues to grow.

John continues to lead mission trips to Asia on a regular basis. Last year he encouraged the principal and administration from his alma mater, Worthington Christian School, to join Asia's Hope on a trip to Cambodia. They returned from that trip with a clear vision of God's heart for the oppressed. Their schools in Columbus, Ohio, signed a multiyear agreement to provide substantial financial, material, and logistical support to Asia's Hope Christian School.

John and Kori are Transformists. Their lives are characterized by obeying God's Word. They love God and love people, and they remain committed to their Christianity and their culture.

But every Transformist looks different because their culture is different. In the next chapter, you'll meet a few more Transformists. Their stories are quite different from the McCollums', but their obedience to God's Word is just as strong—and their impact on the world around them is just as dramatic.

CHAPTER 12

ANGELS DO EXIST

The first time I met Mark Palmer, I was taken aback. Not that I would know, but I guess six-foot-eight probably has that effect on people. Both pastors, we ordered some drinks and told our stories. We talked about philosophy, music, our wives, but mostly about Jesus. Only the way he talked about Jesus was a bit strange. It was as if the Jesus that Mark talked about was real.

Don't get me wrong—I know Jesus is real too, but the stories that Mark shared made it seem like he'd literally spent the day before hanging out with the incarnate Son of God.

I sat there with a barrage of emotions. I felt unsure and confused but mostly intrigued. This guy had a unique quality about him. He wasn't like any other pastor I knew, and I wanted to learn more about him and about his house church—something called the Landing Place, which he referred to as a "missional community."

The plot thickened when Mark handed me his business card. It had a picture of an alien in a spaceship. I looked for his job title, but instead of Pastor, his title read Resident Instigator. And rather than having people refer to him as Mark, his card made it clear he pre-ferred Palmer. Just Palmer.

A few months later I invited Mark to talk to the young adult group at my church. The night of the gathering we wanted our wives to meet, over dinner. Mark, Jennifer, Kelly, and I hit it off. We shared our experiences about life, college, and spirituality. We took turns telling the stories of how we met, fell in love, and got married. Mark and Jennifer told us they were expecting their first child in a few months.

Eventually, we headed over to the young adult gathering where we planned for a Q and A session with the Palmers about their ministry in the Short North neighborhood of Columbus. I hoped our questions would provide a window into how they did church.

A woman named Rachel asked, "What does a typical service look like for you guys?"

"We don't have formal services, at least the way you might normally think of," Mark responded. "We see ourselves as a community of friends and neighbors that 'do life' together. We share a mutual passion for following Jesus."

"That's cool," Rachel commented. "But I guess I'm asking about what activities you guys have in your gathering, like components or something. I mean, you don't just sit in a circle and stare at each other."

"I get what you're asking," Mark said. "We often gather in each other's homes to share meals, have conversations, read Scriptures, tell stories, study the teachings of Jesus, sing songs, pray prayers, recite poetry, and practice liturgies.

"But sometimes," he continued, "a few of us will meet in a coffeehouse or pub for spiritual or philosophical discussions, or we talk about a book we've been reading. We also like to throw worship parties in our art studio. Our parties usually involve candles, incense, loud music, quiet music, visual art, food, sitting, standing, meditation, dialogue, monologue, songs, and ancient prayers."

You could see the wheels turning. For many of us, this was a new way of viewing church. Kyle spoke up. "Do you guys have like a creed or something? I know our church has a statement of faith. Is there something that you guys all agree on biblically?"

"There are certain things we value that shape who we are as a church," Mark said. "First and foremost we value following Jesus. We consider him to not only be the finest teacher that ever lived but also the Messiah. We also value creativity because we're made in the image of the Creator and seek to make him known through our creations."

"So you attract a lot of artists then?" Kyle asked.

"The people who make up the Landing Place are artists, but many are students too. A few attend OSU. Others are thinkers and parents and people who work forty-hour weeks," Mark said.

"Please ... your other values are?" Kyle asked.

"Well, we share life together because life is best experienced together in community," Mark said. "We make peace because Jesus asked us to not only love our friends but also our enemies. Let's see ... we also value the story because in valuing the lives of those who have gone before us we make our own stories richer."

"Wow," said Kyle. "So you guys have like six things you value then?"

"Ummm ... and we live missionally because living as a 'sent' people allows others to see Jesus and experience him for themselves." Mark wasn't used to reducing the Landing Place to a series of belief statements.

I didn't know what everyone else in the room was thinking, but I knew what was going on in my mind. Every time I hung out with Mark, my theology stretched. It was forced out of the box and into real life. I found myself thinking, "That's not the way it's supposed to be done." However, as I compared what he said with the Bible, it was consistent. I guess what gripped me most was the manner in which Mark and Jennifer lived out their faith. This couple was committed to their Christianity and their culture, a daunting task, given their culture. The Short North is Ohio's version of New York's Soho district, a place that values coloring outside the lines—not exactly the easiest place to live out a vibrant faith.

Early Trials

Mark and Jennifer's lives and ministry weren't without obstacles. Some trials came as minor setbacks, and others seemed like overt attacks from the Enemy. Father's Day 2002—Mark's first one as baby Micah's dad—was only the beginning. Mark spent most of that Sunday playing with Micah. The next day he was scheduled to have his colon cancer surgically removed.

The surgery went well. Doctors were able to remove all of the cancer, and they gave him a plan for follow-up care and prevention. Scary stuff for a first-time father in his twenties, but it seemed as if everything was okay. The cancer hadn't slowed Mark down at all.

The Palmers and the Landing Place continued to live out a transformational faith in the Short North. Rather than a program-based church, it seemed to be a people-based church. They were consciously living as Transformists—ministering to the surrounding neighborhoods by meeting needs in extremely practical ways.

I loved what I saw and I wanted a piece of it. I took some teenagers from my church down to pitch in and give them a hand. We painted, cleaned, swept, and organized what Mark called the Kindergarten Room. This space was created as a music venue for the neighborhood, and bands from all over would come and perform. These events were a way to begin a dialogue with neighborhood people. After cleaning up the Kindergarten Room, we set up shop on the Palmers' front porch and cooked hot dogs for neighbors and strangers who passed by.

One of the things I liked about the Palmers was that they actually tried to live what they preached. When they talked about a life of simplicity without excessive possessions, they responded by reducing their inventory and selling much of what they had. After they explored what the Bible said about hospitality, they responded by welcoming others into their household. Their life of faith consisted of studying God's Word and then obeying God's Word, something characteristic of all Transformists.

But living out their faith wasn't always easy. For the Palmers, following Jesus had a real cost. It meant life change, something which isn't always popular. Not all Transformists look—or should look—like the Palmers. Yet all Transformists obey Jesus when he speaks. They follow him wherever he calls.

Mark was an avid reader, not only of the Scriptures but also of Christian classics. He constantly challenged his mind with new thoughts, models, and mandates. He had a love for literature and often led his community into rediscovering some of the greats. In late 2002 he was trying to digest Dietrich Bonhoeffer's *The Cost of Discipleship*, and it wasn't going down smoothly.

Mark asked, "Why are we, the church, constantly asking questions like 'How do we make it easier for people to hear the gospel?' or 'How can we create a better or more comfortable introduction to Jesus?' Jesus never said that it would be easy or comfortable to follow him, so why are we trying so hard to make it so? Could it be that our efforts to make the gospel more palatable have led to the anemic state of the church today? Have we castrated the Son of God in our attempt to make him more 'seeker-friendly'?"

Mark's evaluation was more than just theory; his comments concerning Bonhoeffer's *Cost of Discipleship* were made just after the church had been robbed. The week before, the Kindergarten Room was broken into. The Landing Place lost over six thousand dollars' worth of equipment. Mark immediately sent out an update to all those who followed their ministry in the Short North:

In order to move forward, we desperately need your prayers. Please pray for protection, and for the recovery of the items that were stolen. Pray that the Kingdom will advance in Urban Columbus. Pray that the Holy Spirit will give us hearts of mercy and forgiveness. Pray that those who took the items would somehow fall in love with Jesus and be radically transformed. Saint Paul said, "Don't let evil get the best of you, but conquer evil by doing good." All praise and honor to Jesus the Christ.

About a week later their faith was tested again when they were robbed for the second time. What I appreciate about Mark is his authenticity. This time he was ticked and wasn't afraid to admit it. Being a Transformist means being real, so when Satan kicked Mark to the curb, Mark made it clear he didn't like it.

"The Kindergarten Room is pretty much out of business," he said. "I thought it was pretty cool while it lasted. The thing that I don't get is that you move into a neighborhood, try to do something good for that neighborhood, to better it, and the neighbors just kick you and take your stuff."

The next step, as it always is for a Transformist, is to keep walking the fine line. God doesn't mind our anger or our doubt—but he does want us to keep on walking. And this is exactly what Mark did.

The Two Became One

In the spring of 2003, Mark told me that Jennifer was experiencing pain in her stomach. Confirmation soon came: Jennifer had stomach cancer.

From the first day of the diagnosis, the Palmers believed that God could supernaturally heal Jennifer. Believing in the power of prayer, the Palmers asked their friends to share Jennifer's story with their networks of relationships and encourage them to pray as well.

The news was shocking, especially because Jennifer was only twenty-six years old and the mother of a toddler. Mark and Jennifer were good people, doing so much for their community — striving to be relevant, to love God and people. About a week after the news hit, Mark wrestled with the possible outcomes concerning this type of cancer. Fear was setting in.

He said he was frightened that he might have to spend the rest of his life without his best friend and lover. He was frightened that Micah would never know his mother. He was frightened about all the pain that Jennifer would face and that his family would not be able to cope with the emotional and physical toll that cancer brings.

More quickly than he could anticipate, some of Mark's fears came true. In late April, Jennifer had surgery and doctors discovered tumors had spread across her entire abdomen. The cancer was so extensive that there was no course of treatment. They placed a tube in Jennifer's stomach to drain fluid and provide her a little comfort, and then they closed her up.

Mark shared the startling reality. "There is really nothing they can do at this point. The doctors say she has a few months left to live."

In the midst of this, Mark tried to cling to a divine perspective. "All of this has changed nothing in regard to who God is and what he is able to do. We simply find ourselves in a position where only a direct and miraculous act of the Father will change the situation. God knows that Micah and I are not ready to give up our mother and wife. But in reality, she is not ours to give up — she is God's. She is his and he will care for her."

God seemed committed to remind the Palmers that he loved them and knew about their pain. Throughout Jennifer's terminal illness, followers of Christ were present in amazing ways, providing money, meals, and prayer. These tangible acts of grace were a strong reminder that they were not alone.

Mark no longer took anything for granted, savoring every moment as sacred. Two daily events meant the world to him. "The first event begins my day," Mark explained. "It's waking up for the first time in the early morning and touching Jennifer's hand, to feel its warmth. I touch her chest to feel the gentle rise and fall of it. The rhythm of her breathing has become familiar in the last five years; I sense I will never forget that particular rhythm. I then lay quietly for as long as I like and simply watch her sleep."

"The second event ends my day," Mark said. "It is the act of putting my fifteen-month-old son Micah to bed. After bath time, we rock a bit and sing. We talk of the future. I tell him in as many different ways as I know how that he means everything to me. I pray, asking God to make him a prophet in the tradition of his namesake. I pray Jennifer's prayer for him, that he will love his enemies as much as he loves his neighbors. We cuddle. And then with a goodnight kiss, I lay him to sleep. This event closes my day and completes it."

Mark had the wisdom to know that both of these events — like all things in life — would not last forever, but that didn't make it any easier to let go.

A Long Summer

In the summer of 2003, Jennifer was in the midst of her second round of chemotherapy. She had some additional CT scans, the first ones since the beginning of her treatment. The scans showed the worst. The cancer had doubled in size and aggressively spread throughout other areas of her body.

Because of the bad report, Jennifer would not continue her current form of treatment, and the doctors didn't want her to eat any longer, fearing possible damage to her digestive system. As a result, Jennifer was admitted to the hospital to receive nutrition fed through a central line in her chest.

The news was incredibly disappointing.

Still the Palmers remained hopeful. Mark confessed, "God's will is still for Jennifer to be completely whole and healthy and disease-free. That is his will for all of his children. Jennifer's news doesn't change the fact that the death and resurrection of Jesus of Nazareth two thousand years ago provided for not only our spiritual healing but for our physical as well."

Despite Mark's and Jennifer's faith, her illness was wearing on them. Mark reached an emotional low in July. "Have you ever watched your twenty-six-year-old wife squirm in complete agony, calling out to God to take away her pain, only to have it grow worse?" The next evening, at about midnight, they took Jennifer to the emergency room. Morphine was the only thing that would relieve her pain.

About a week later the Palmers were able to get a short break from doctors and hospitals. They took a trip to Cincinnati, where they joined friends from around the region for a time of worship. Throughout their season in ministry, these regional gatherings were a critical time that fed their souls. No matter how poorly she felt, Jennifer didn't want to miss this gathering. Mark was encouraged that weekend, seeing Jennifer bathed in prayer by so many people who loved her.

But the Monday after, the cancer lashed out again. The entire week was torture for Jennifer. Finally, on Sunday, she returned to the emergency room. While there, waste began to drain from the tube in her stomach—Jennifer's stomach and bowels had fused together, and waste could now pass freely into her abdomen.

Jennifer stopped receiving nutrition, since it was only feeding the tumors and making her sicker. And so it was that Mark brought Jennifer home so she could be comfortable during her last days. At home they controlled the constant pain with injections. Sometimes Jennifer was aware, and sometimes she wasn't, yet the Landing Place continued with the regular gatherings.

On the first of August, at one such gathering, Jennifer was too weak to come downstairs, so the community went up to her. They gathered in the entryway, in the stairway, and in the hall that led to her bedroom. They sang to her and she joined in on the chorus:

> *Rejoice, lift up your voice and praise Jesus now.*
> *Hallelujah.*
> *Our Father in Heaven, holy is Your name.*
> *Your Kingdom come, your will be done here.*[1]

When they were done singing, Mark whispered to Jennifer that what she had just experienced was a tiny taste of the kingdom to come. She smiled.

Eleven days later, in the morning, Jennifer went to be with her Father God. Mark made the announcement in an email: "Jennifer's physical body awaits the resurrection of the dead on the day of the Lord. We live this life to the glory of God. We anxiously wait for the next life to begin. All praise to Jesus of Nazareth, the Resurrected One."

Life after Death

The first night after Jennifer's death was a trial for Mark. "I am frightened of going upstairs to bed by myself," he confided. "I have gone to sleep with Jennifer every night for the last five-plus years, and now I am quite unsure of how to do it by myself." He asked people to pray with him through the night, and thirty-eight people posted a message to Mark before the sun rose again.

About a week and a half later, Mark told me about small things that triggered memories of his wife, things like receiving junk mail addressed to Jennifer or finding a strand of her hair on a pillow. Grief blindsided Mark. Even a casual trip to Lowe's was marked by sadness because the nice cashier gave Micah a flower "to take home to your mommy."

Mark needed to get away. He needed time to heal, and so a couple of weeks after the funeral he headed west and spent some time with a few dear friends. Although he missed his son dearly, Micah's grandparents kept him occupied on their three acres in the Pennsylvania hills.

In his grief, Mark asked some hard questions:

Why did God reveal the source of Jennifer's sickness without giving them what they needed to defeat it?

Why did Jennifer's battle end the way that it did?

Why did she suffer and why was God silent?

What do these things reveal about who God is?

By pushing so hard against the pseudo-kingdom of Satan, had he put Jennifer in harm's way?

Would Jennifer have gotten sick if they would have been satisfied with a blasé Christian existence?

Mark didn't worry if people believed such questions were disrespectful or even blasphemous. He thought it was disrespectful and blasphemous *not* to ask them. But to his disappointment, Mark didn't get many answers and, instead, his sadness grew ever greater. He wished the grief would either leave him or refine him, but at the moment all it seemed to be doing was eating away at his insides little by little. Mark admitted, "My future hope is in the resurrection of the dead, and a reunion with Jennifer in the kingdom fully come. But my present hope is a bit more elusive right now."

Friends from the Landing Place ministered to Mark in a special way over the next few months. These were Jennifer's friends too, and so as Mark spent time with them they brought a certain sense of comfort. That October four of them—Amy, Kelli, Tawd, and Jeremy—took Mark to hear Copeland, one of his favorite bands.

The band held a distinctive place in his heart because their album had spoken to him and to Jennifer as they journeyed through her battle with cancer. That night Mark came away from the show with mixed emotions — sadness, anger, joy, and a sense of healing. One song was particularly significant. Mark felt as if the lyrics described the circumstances of Jennifer's last days in the hospital — he was her angel wanting so badly to take her pain away.

> *There's an angel by your hospital bed*
> *Desperate to hear his name on your breath*
> *As he looks down you're not making a sound*
> *Open your eyes look at me*
> *I'll bring to you whatever you need*
> *And I'll tell you I'm sorry*
> *That I can't take this pain away from you*
> *And put it on my own body if I knew how to …*
> *It's testing the strong ones*
> *Scarring the beautiful ones*
> *It's holding the loved ones*
> *One last time*[2]

Strangely, eighteen months later, these circumstances would be repeated in a similar fashion. This time Mark wouldn't be *by* the hospital bed; he would be *in* it. Stranger yet, his angel was with him at the concert that evening. He just didn't know it at the time.

Time Heals, Sometimes Slowly

Mark continued to grieve throughout the autumn months. At times it seemed like his sorrow increased rather than decreased. Friends told him to rake leaves or take Micah to the park or get some sleep. These ideas provided Mark a brief detachment from his grief, but it was the Landing Place that offered him comfort. Providentially, the relief was so significant that he wondered aloud, "How do people who have suffered loss continue to function without a community like mine?"

One of Mark's friends suggested that every night before bed he should make a list of five things that were really good about that particular day. He figured that maybe the list would help Mark with his overall feelings of grief and hopelessness.

The idea didn't work, but it gave Mark another idea. He decided to make a list of five things that angered him beyond his ability to handle. Here was the list he came up with:

1. Judgmental "Christians" who think they have it all figured out, when in reality they have almost nothing figured out, which is ironic since they spend the majority of their time attempting to force the minutia of their religion down the throats of those who would probably be really interested in giving their whole lives to Jesus if it weren't for these "Christians."

2. When "Christians," through their words and actions, swear allegiance to the kingdom of this world, thus denying everything that Jesus said and did.

3. When "Christians" live as if the kingdom of God is a place that you go when you die instead of a present reality that demands singular allegiance.

4. Death, especially of unborn children and twenty-six-year-old wives and mothers.

5. How quickly 1 thru 4 cause me to sin by being filled with anger.

The Cold Melts

The Christmas season was exceptionally difficult for Mark. He asked, "How can I continue to do what I do without Jennifer? She was my confidant; I don't have one anymore. She was my best friend; no one has become that, nor could they if they tried. She was everything that I am not. I am now half the person I was—probably more like a quarter of the person I was. She completed me like no one else will ever be able to."

One Friday night Mark wasn't doing well. Micah was asleep and the house was empty. Mark wrote in his journal, "I am unsure of what I'm supposed to do with all this silence and solitude. I've forgotten how to be alone. It might be best if I relearn the skill."

Different people from the Landing Place ministered to Mark in a variety of ways. Some hung out with Mark. Others made meals. And still others babysat Micah so that Mark had time to fulfill his "pastoral" duties with the community. One young woman named Amy, a friend of Mark and Jennifer, did just this. Amy's care for Micah allowed Mark some rare and much-needed time to cultivate his mind and spirit.

The New Year brought grief and hope with it. That January the Landing Place decided that instead of writing resolutions, they would write prayers instead. Mark's prayer sounded like something right out of the psalms: "Oh Father distant and near (can I still call you that?), I cry to you with insides buried by soil, with one lung exploded from breathing air stained by death and the grave."

Mark posted many of his thoughts in an online journal. Hundreds of people followed the Palmer story, as evidenced from the emails they sent. These emails assured Mark, Micah, and the Landing Place that they were all being lifted up in prayer on a daily basis.

Requests for Mark to share his story began to come in from various churches and youth groups. It seemed like other followers of Jesus wanted to hear the story of how Mark was persevering through trials. His travels were painful, but he felt they were necessary. He wasn't sharing easy answers or feel-good theology—he was offering his broken heart to other people and to God.

Cultivating the Mind and the Heart

In the spring, Mark was still going through some tough times. He felt like the "worst 'church planter' that ever lived." He sensed the possibility of his dreams dying. One evening his heaviness reached a new low, and he needed someone to lift him from the pit he was in. That person was Amy. She reminded Mark of the many people who loved him. She reminded him of his beautiful son, who thought the sun rose and set with him. She assured him that God would do something through him despite all of his perceived "inadequacies."

Mark seemed to experience healing when he was with Amy and Micah. God showed him that because he could be called father, friend, and spiritual director, he was a rich man. These realizations were clearer after a week spent napping, walking, and rafting in Pennsylvania with Amy, Micah, and Mark's parents.

Mark remembered Jennifer the most when he was with Micah. He could see her when he looked deep into Micah's eyes. When Mark held Micah, he said he "could almost smell her." And when Micah gave Mark a big hug, it was as if he was hugging her once again.

June 20, 2004, would have been Mark's and Jennifer's six-year wedding anniversary. It fell on Father's Day. On that particular summer day, Amy came over early to get Micah up so Mark could sleep in. Then they all went outside to work in the gardens that Mark made for Jennifer. The day of work in the sunshine ended with Dr. Seuss books and silly songs with Micah.

Mark missed Jennifer terribly. He longed to be reunited with her and believed with everything in him that one day he would be. It's what gave him hope. But although Mark grieved the past, he also lived in the present. As always, he was willing and open to what God had planned, no matter where it led. As a Transformist he considered obeying God's Word his highest calling. In early August, Mark felt the freedom to announce this to his friends and family via email:

Amy has been a part of our community for a few years; she was friends with both Jennifer and me, and spoke at Jennifer's memorial service. After Jennifer passed away, she really began to care for Micah in a very special way, and in so doing cared for me as well. As the months passed, we became better and better friends, until it was obvious that God was bringing us together in a very unique and redemptive way. She has been and is an amazing woman. I love her with all of my heart, with all of my soul, with all of my strength, and on November 6th I will be married to my best friend Amy Smith.

The Landing Place was thrilled that their spiritual director had discovered a best friend who would complement him in life and ministry. However, Amy's mom was unsettled with the idea of her daughter marrying Mark. She prayed about this unrest in her soul. Driving home one day, she felt the Lord tell her, "This marriage isn't about Amy. It's about Mark. She is being called to serve." She had no idea how true those words would become.

Rebirth

As the months passed, Mark underwent a gentle transformation. He smiled more. Amy was becoming part of his and Micah's lives. They couldn't wait for her to move in—saying good-bye every night was getting old for Mark.

Mark was proud of Amy. His heart had found love again, and he wasn't afraid to let the world know. He unashamedly posted his affection for her in his online journal:

I think this goes without saying, but most of you probably don't know her, so I'll say it anyway ... I really am marrying an amazing woman. Amy has been my best friend for some time now, and she has been everything one could ask for in a best friend.

She has supported me in all that I do (and attempt to do), she encourages me ceaselessly, she is a wonderful mother to Micah (he loves her deeply), she is a guide to me in my life of discipleship ... I'm only scratching the surface of her depth and beauty. I am so blessed to be marrying this girl in thirty days. What a beautiful twist to the story.

Mark was in tune with the reality that God was writing a story. He knew that nothing in life was by accident and all of life was leading toward the eventual fullness of Jesus' kingdom. Mark characterized his marriage to Amy as a "beautiful twist." Their story would experience many more twists in the near future, although not all would be beautiful.

About two weeks before the wedding, Mark went to the hospital to get X-rays on his back. He'd been having pain for about five months and the pain medication was no longer helping. Doctors wanted to get a closer look. Mark didn't hide the fact that he hated hospitals as they brought back a lot of memories, most of them not pleasant.

One might wonder what was going through Micah's mind at this time. What would a two-and-a-half-year-old think of all these transitions? Mark told a story that provided some insight.

"This morning I called Micah over and picked him up and put him on my lap. I wanted to try to explain the excitement of his daddy getting married to Amy in two weeks. So I said to him, 'Micah, you know that daddy and Amy are getting married in two weeks?' He said, 'Yep!' I asked him, 'Is that okay with you?' He replied with another enthusiastic 'Yep!' Well, this was going well, so I decided to go a bit deeper with the next question. 'Do you know what that means?' I asked. Without hesitation, Micah answered, 'Yeah, presents!'"

My wife, Kelly, and I considered ourselves blessed to have attended the wedding—a beautiful, amazing celebration characterized with rich Jewish overtones. Although risky in November, Mark and Amy decided to have an outdoor evening wedding in an elegant, spacious tent. Seating was extremely tight, proving the fact that they were loved by many.

Their story was a testimony to God's faithfulness and the rebirth that he often initiates in our lives. Mark wore deep joy on his face that evening. Because of Jennifer's passing he seemed to know the brevity of life in a way many of us never acknowledge until it's too late, and thus he was fully present that evening.

The newlyweds sped off to Canada for their honeymoon, complete with blue skies and crisp mountain air. Mark and Amy hiked, soaked in the hot springs, and saw breathtaking views from a gondola. But their paradise was cut short.

The Tragic Truth

Right after the honeymoon, Mark had an MRI to determine the cause of his continuing back pain. A couple days later the doctor's office called. The results were in. He needed to discuss them with the doctor that afternoon. Mark called Amy at work. He was extremely upset, so she left work to join him for lunch. He said the doctors believed the back pain was due to a degenerative disc disorder.

Mark thought otherwise. He let Amy into his private fear. "Amy, I think my back pain might be cancer. Maybe God had us get married so that you could be Micah's mom."

After lunch Mark and Amy headed to the doctor's office to discuss the MRI results. The doctor asked Mark when he had his last colonoscopy. He went on to explain that at times cancer can present itself as back pain. Mark and Amy left the office that day with a treatment plan to deal with the back pain. Mark also left with the possibility of another diagnosis, one he didn't want to focus on.

Later in December, Mark took his first ride in an ambulance. He had trouble breathing, and he couldn't feel his arms or legs. The doctors diagnosed his sickness as pneumonia.

Despite Mark's growing physical pain, he decided to start working toward a graduate degree, an MA in New Testament at Ashland Theological Seminary. He saw this as a small step in achieving a greater goal of earning a PhD and one day teaching at a university. Amy, as usual, supported Mark in his dream.

Mark's pain continued to worsen during those first few weeks of January. He felt extremely guilty. There was not one day in the previous four months that he didn't have back pain. He thought it was wearing on Amy. She not only cared for him every day but she also heard his complaints.

But it soon turned out that Mark was justified in complaining. His back pain was being treated as a disk protrusion and arthritis, but a CT scan revealed a tumor behind his rectum that was pressing against his spine.

The news came as a shock, but Mark and Amy were filled with confidence and peace. Immediately, they began to solicit prayers, asking people to join them in the fight.

Mark knew the news had a huge impact on Amy. He worried about her. He couldn't imagine the stress of being a new wife, a new mother, working full time, and now, on top of it all, having to take care of a very sick husband. He knew she was tired, frustrated, and sad.

The Palmers believed that the cancer was an opportunity to see the kingdom come among them. They were confident that the combination of prayer and the skill of the doctors would bring about a positive ending to their story.

Mark soon felt the effects of the diagnosis and the chemo. He canceled a speaking trip and resigned from a leadership position. "It saddens me greatly. I hope there won't be many more things that this cursed disease takes from me. I'm ready to start treatment and fry this tumor."

Time to Pay Up

Mark didn't like to talk about money. The truth is his medical procedures were quite expensive, and, to make matters worse, his health-sharing group decided not to cover any of the medical bills for his treatment. With costs exceeding $75,000, things looked grim. Mark knew only one way to bypass all the medical bills. He prayed for "that way" to be accomplished.

He prayed to be healed.

He knew medical bills could be a huge blow to his family, one that would be difficult to recover from. Yet if God chose not to heal him, he believed the kingdom "erupted into" even things like money. The Palmers placed their hope in the kingdom and the King.

Mark's surgery went well, relatively speaking. But while the doctors were removing the tumor, they found that the cancer had spread to his liver. The doctor removed the small tumor on his liver and felt confident he had removed all the cancer. It meant that Mark's chemotherapy might be a little more intense.

They waited for Mark's bowels to start working. The doctors inserted a tube to start draining his stomach. Mark was extremely uncomfortable. He said at times God seemed absent from that hospital room, but everybody's prayers brought him through.

Two weeks after the surgery, the Palmers received some major news. They saw prayers answered right before their eyes. The hospital made the commitment to cover 100 percent of Mark's treatment within their facility up until a certain point. However, Mark needed to reapply every three months, which meant the surgery was not technically covered yet.

Additional CT scans revealed that Mark had three more cancer spots on his liver—more surgery and chemo were looming. Many people decided to fast and pray for Mark. His prayer was that he would return home soon.

But Mark wouldn't be home soon. He entered into what seemed like the valley of the shadow of death.

Forty-nine days later, he finally wrote on his online journal. Mark was supposed to be hospitalized for surgery for only seven days. He had gone into liver failure after the surgery and almost died. He had no memory of days fourteen to twenty-one due to a second surgery and an overdose on pain killers. Without the second surgery, he would have died. Mark said it was humbling to think about. For whatever reason, his life was spared for the time being. He believed God had more for him to do.

Amy became Micah's mother on September 12. Although she had been his mother for quite a long time, the adoption made it official. It was a happy day for many reasons. Mark felt odd saying it, but he sensed the Holy Spirit was present that day in the courtroom, and it brought peace to his spirit knowing that if anything ever happened to him, Micah would have an amazing woman to raise him.

September brought with it more encouragement. Some followers of Jesus in Pewaukee, Wisconsin, had a monster yard sale to raise money for Mark's medical bills. Mark had only met three or four of the people involved. The sale was spearheaded by, in Mark's words, "a crazy/reckless/passionate/visionary guy named Jim Watters" and the little kingdom community that met in his house.

The same kind of thing happened in the little town that Mark grew up in and he was sure in many other places he didn't even know about. Mark saw all this generosity and kindness as God's redemption of a horrible and evil situation. Because of his cancer, people were learning to live and function as communities. Mark said, "If God is using my illness to spread the ideals of the kingdom, then I will gladly bear this pain."

A couple weeks later Mark got the results back from his most recent CT scan and it revealed that he had a new spot of cancer on his liver as well as a spot on his right lung. Strangely, Mark felt the need to encourage his online readers, just in case they were tempted to lose heart. He remained steadfast:

> Be hopeful. Don't stop fighting. On some level this thing is bigger than all of us. It's not about having a wife die of cancer at twenty-six, and then two years later getting the same terminal illness. It's not about me and how I fight this disease or how our little family walks through it. The bigger picture is the battle against sickness and death that we all face because we live in a broken world. But it's even more about the kingdom that has broken in and offers us a chance at relief from that disease. It offers health and victory where before there was none. There is hope in the midst of hopelessness. Death is not where we lose; the onset of hopelessness is the great defeater. So allow hope to rise up within you.

On their one-year wedding anniversary, Mark and Amy invited the Landing Place community over for a party. Their spiritual family journeyed with them every step of this first unbelievable year of marriage, and it was only fitting that they celebrate with them.

At the gathering Mark even wore a tie. The food was from Aladdin's, the wine from Gentiles, and the music by Mike. Yet all these components paled in comparison to the richness of sharing that night with their community, making it Mark's favorite weekend of the year.

About a week later the couple got each other anniversary presents: new tattoos, Amy's first and Mark's third.

It was Amy's idea. She got the word "hope" in Hebrew, symbolically placed on her chest where Mark's medi-port was located. This was the port where Mark received all of his chemo. He got the word "hope" in Greek on his forearm, with an image of a tree growing up out of it. The tree was inspired by Ezekiel 47:1 – 12.

A few days later the Palmers' friend Aaron put on a benefit show to raise money for Mark's medical bills. The Landing Place booked the bands, cooked the food, and provided housing and hospitality. The entire evening was another act of love given on behalf of the Palmers. Believers from all over poured out their love, compassion, and generosity. Checks were sent from all over the world, some big, some small. Each email, gift, and prayer reminded the Palmers of the Father's love and convinced them that God had not forgotten them.

One particular gift stood out.

After returning home from a wonderful day with his wife, Mark found a used copy of *Divine Disobedience* on his pillow in the bedroom. He took only a quick look at it because there were friends downstairs waiting for him to play cards. Later, Amy came down and asked if he knew anything about the book on the bed. Mark said he had glanced at it. She told him there was an envelope inside containing a very large amount of cash. There was no note, no indication of who it was from. Just a used book filled with money and encouragement.

Reality

The end of December brought both good news and bad news. The most recent scan showed that the spot on Mark's liver was gone and the spot on his lung had greatly decreased in size. The bad news: there was a mass on Mark's rectum at the site where the whole ordeal began, where the tumor had caused the extreme pain in his tailbone.

In his online journal, Mark apologized that his news wasn't any better. Although he admitted to his online readers that the cancer battle can get tiring, he asked them not to give up on him and reminded them their prayers were critical.

At times God used Micah to get Mark through the downs. One bedtime exchange was particularly encouraging:

Daddy: I'm so glad we're all back home together.
Micah: I know. I missed you.
Daddy: You did? Why did you miss me?
Micah: Because I love you.
Daddy: I love you too, little man.

Mark soon stopped writing in his online journal, and Amy took over for him—not a good sign. In response to the nausea and stomach pain, Mark went to the hospital in mid-March. His bowels also were inconsistent, sometimes working and other times failing. The doctors tried, ever so slowly, to reintroduce food into his system.

That week my parents came from Wisconsin to visit their new grandson, Keegan. Spring peeked through on that twentieth day of March, and the sun initiated a much-anticipated winter thaw. Kelly stayed with Keegan while my mom, my dad, and I went to visit the Palmers in the hospital.

When I opened the door to Mark's room, I was immediately taken aback and part of me wished I had never turned that knob. I couldn't believe how famished Mark looked. Undeniably, my once healthy, robust friend was on his deathbed, his body ravaged by cancer.

Mark introduced us to his parents, Vivian and Dick. His mom said something that afternoon which continues to ring in my mind today. In praising Amy, Vivian proudly said to us, "We believe Amy was sent to be Mark's angel. She was placed in his life at exactly the right time. God was involved in every facet of their relationship ... the way they met. Amy never dated before Mark. The Lord was preparing her for this."

I turned to Amy. She smiled but looked away, embarrassed by the heartfelt compliments. She sat next to Mark's hospital bed, holding his hand. The whole scene was a manifestation of the Copeland tune from the concert Mark and Amy attended in October 2003.

Although incredibly weak, Mark strained his voice to tell us about a new strategy for his recovery. We prayed for the Palmers, and his dad walked us out of the room. Circumstances would change drastically just a week later.

Mark came home from the hospital and, although feeling incredibly weak, he couldn't wait to celebrate Micah's fourth birthday at a local bowling alley with family and friends. After the party, back at the Palmer house, Mark sat in a chair while Micah opened his presents.

The next day, Sunday, was a difficult one for Mark. He was weak and couldn't move, and his body was shutting down, making it impossible to eat. That evening the Landing Place had a gathering. They decided to have it at the Palmers' house in order to be near their spiritual director. Mark stayed upstairs, not wanting to be near anybody.

Amy was torn, not wanting the cancer to take Mark away from the community. She asked Mark if he was okay if people came upstairs in pairs to pray over him. He agreed.

Around nine that night things got worse. Amy was getting worried about Mark's deteriorating condition, and she begged him to sit up in bed. With his head on her shoulder he said, "Amy, I need to go to the hospital."

She expressed her concern. "I don't want you to. I'm afraid you won't come back home."

Seeing her pain, Mark asked if she had lost hope. She said no, and Mark said, "If you've lost hope, I could die right now."

Amy asked Mark's dad to dial 911 because she didn't have the strength. The ambulance arrived, and paramedics carried Mark down the stairs. Amy stayed next to him on the way to the hospital and into the ICU. "I love you and Jesus is here with you," she told him.

Although he didn't have the strength to reply, his eyes reassured her that he understood.

The entire Landing Place community came to the hospital to

be at his side that morning. Amy called his name and Mark briefly opened his eyes. They sang three songs: "Nothing But the Blood of Jesus," "Let Your Glory Fall," and "Our Father." Mark's father read Psalm 23.

Then Mark's heart stopped.

That morning Amy wrote in her journal:

I loved Mark with my whole being ... we loved each other. We both found love when we weren't expecting it. I don't think my love for him will ever die. Although I'm in extreme pain, I must be strong for Micah. When I look at him, I see Mark and Jennifer. I have so many questions ... I had hope until his last breath. Please remember Mark ... he was an amazing teacher, student, and leader. He was a fantastic lover and husband. He was the best father anybody could ask for. I'm not quite ready to give him up, I probably never will. Please pray for me ... memories are really hard for me. I am very sentimental. Mark fought the battle well.

March 27 was the longest day of Amy's entire life. The evening wasn't any easier. Sadly, her journal entry sounded strangely familiar, like one Mark had written a couple years prior:

Please pray for me as I go to sleep tonight. It is hard for me to sleep in this bed alone ... without Mark's hand to hold or his warm body to make me feel secure. This room is difficult, but I do feel a sense of peace here. I just keep thinking he will walk through the door or that he is here next to me.

Amy had to tell Micah about his daddy. He didn't really understand at first, but finally Micah said, "After a long, long time, I will see him."

Amy's heart broke.

Three days later, Amy buried her lover.

The funeral was extremely emotional. We shared story after story. One girl communicated her sorrow through an interpretive dance dedicated to Mark. We sang songs. We prayed. We gave Jesus glory that we all were able to share life with Mark and Amy.

After the funeral, the Palmer home was full of friends, food, and conversation. The Landing Place community grieved and celebrated the passing of their spiritual director. Amy's job quickly switched from caring for Mark to caring for Micah. That first night after the funeral, Amy tried to comfort Micah. She found him crying in his sleep. He missed his daddy.

Life after Death, Again

Life moved on, again, as it always must. A couple of weeks later Amy went to Mansfield, Pennsylvania. Amy's mom accompanied her and Micah on their trip to visit Mark's family. Amy found some time to be alone and journal, and she found herself at a coffee shop, tears streaming down her face.

She longed for Mark—for his touch, his voice, his presence. The Lord seemed to be silent. She couldn't hear or feel him. When Mark took his last breath, the Lord too became silent.

Amy tried to be strong for Micah. His young mind seemed to grasp the cold reality of Mark's departure. One day while in Pennsylvania they both were looking at pictures of Mark. Amy showed Micah a picture from the wedding. She asked him where daddy was and he said, "With Jesus." Another day they watched videos of Mark playing basketball. Micah cheered every time Mark scored a basket.

Amy and Micah were good for each other. They helped each other grieve. Amy said that Micah was Mark's greatest gift to her. She never thought she would be a single mother and would often tell Mark that she had no interest in being one. But Micah was the only thing that kept her going. Every night she told him that he was her favorite little boy in the whole world. She loved being his mom, and they learned together what it meant to continue on with life.

Amy received her first tattoo, the word *Hope*, with Mark for their one-year wedding anniversary. When they left the tattoo parlor that day Mark said, "It would be cool if you got the word *Healed* when I am healed."

Throughout Mark's sickness, Amy thought about his comment. Things changed when Mark died. Amy could no longer hope for his healing, but for the resurrection. So in June of 2006 she got her second tattoo, the word *Resurrection*. Now both of her tattoos, Hope and Resurrection, are a constant reminder of where her hope lies.

The first Father's Day without Mark was difficult. Amy often thought about Mark's love and commitment to Micah. In her mind, it was best illustrated the day of Micah's birthday party at the bowling alley. It took every ounce of strength for Mark to get there.

Mark often asked Amy if she thought Micah would remember him if the cancer would take him from this world. Amy told Mark she would make sure that Micah did remember by keeping his memory alive.

On the anniversary of Jennifer's death, Amy visited her grave. She wept and read a poem that Mark would often read. She sat there for a while and prayed.

Then she moved a few feet from Jennifer's grave to Mark's. She wept and questioned God. Why did both of them have to suffer and die like they did? Why did all of this happen? Jennifer's illness consumed Amy's prayers and thoughts. She wanted so much to see her healed. And then Mark's illness consumed Amy's life too. She thought God would heal him.

Both Mark's and Jennifer's lives live on through Micah, Amy, and the Landing Place. Someday they will all once again take part in one of their favorite things: a meal around the table with family and friends.

More Miracles

Life is still difficult for Amy, Micah, and the Landing Place. They've lost their lover, their father, and their spiritual director. Yet God is faithful.

The Palmer family incurred over $600,000 more in medical bills as a result of Mark's illness. Many people chipped away at that insurmountable amount. As a result, they paid off around $75,000 during his treatments. However, the remaining balance was quite a burden for a single mom. For six months, Amy called the hospital frequently and mailed every necessary piece of information requested, trying to fulfill the requirements for coverage.

On October 10, 2006, the hospital called to inform her that they were approved for 100 percent coverage. Amy said Mark had "unwavering faith that the bills would either be forgiven or that we would be able to pay them somehow."

God miraculously answered Mark's request about the bills. And one day he will answer Mark's ultimate request: bodily resurrection.

I wrote the Palmers' story for one reason: that our generation might have the opportunity to see inside the lives of a few Transformists. Their trials revealed what many of us already knew about them. They remained relevant in their faith, committed to their Christianity and their culture.

They lived out the paradox of being in the world but not of it.

They discovered the secret of the fine line.

They found the kingdom.

CHAPTER 13

THY KINGDOM COME

"These verses aren't for us today," my Bible teacher explained. "Jesus' Sermon on the Mount paints a picture of how the world will operate one day in the millennial kingdom."

And so began my misconception of the kingdom that "misled" me well into my adulthood. Supposedly people like my Bible teacher believed that the lifestyle and ethic Jesus called people to in the Sermon on the Mount is impossible within our present time and, therefore, it must be for a future time.

I'm not afraid to admit it: the Sermon on the Mount contains some startling commands. Like Matthew 5:40: "If someone wants to sue you and take your tunic, let him have your cloak as well." Or Matthew 5:42: "Give to the one who asks you, and do not turn away from the one who wants to borrow from you." Or Matthew 5:48: "Be perfect, therefore, as your heavenly Father is perfect." No wonder we look for ways to get ourselves off the hook of following these difficult sayings. We toss out rationalizations: "Maybe they're metaphors." "Maybe they're about some future time." "Maybe they're just suggestions."

I think it's Christians who live like they're "off the hook" who caused people like Mahatma Gandhi to become critical of our religion. He saw a disconnection between the way Jesus lived and the way Christians live. Because of this Gandhi said, "If it weren't for Christians, I'd be a Christian." Gandhi didn't disagree with Jesus' teachings. He went on record to say, "I like your Christ, but I don't like your Christians." And those of us who know Gandhi's story understand the sobering reality that he embodied the ethics described by Jesus in the Sermon on the Mount better than most Christians.

Perhaps one reason for these embarrassing disconnections between belief and action is because of our view of the Sermon on the Mount. If we don't believe it's for us, then we don't have to live it, and if we don't live it, then we're irrelevant. And being irrelevant destroys the possibility of living as Transformists.

So is the sermon for us today?

The answer is "yes" and "no."

Jesus' first coming introduced us into a new age, a kingdom age, which Jesus referred to as the kingdom of heaven or kingdom of God. It's how he lived and it's what he preached. Jesus said, "I must preach the good news of the kingdom of God to the other towns also, because that is why I was sent" (Luke 4:43). But even though the kingdom of God is for today, it isn't yet here in its fullness. We are in a fallen world, and we are sinners saved by grace. So, Jesus' sermon is for today *and* Jesus' sermon is for the future kingdom.

Acknowledging that the kingdom of God is present today — but not yet here in its fullness — is called an "already/not yet" view of the kingdom. This view admits the obvious tension that exists. Believers expect to see God actively working in the world today, at times through healing, miracles, and direct intervention because the kingdom of God is already here. And yet because the kingdom of God is not here in its full manifestation, sin, evil, and darkness march on but not as unrestricted as they would without the kingdom of God.[1]

Why is all this talk of the kingdom important?

The kingdom is critical if we want to transform our world. Transformists are an entire group who live according to these different rules. We take the words of Jesus literally, in their proper context, even when it's inconvenient.

When you meet someone who operates according to a different set of rules, it tends to make you stop and take notice. I remember one time Mark Palmer and I planned to hang out. I met him at his house before we headed over to Haiku, one of his favorite restaurants. I hopped into his vehicle and commented that I liked it. He turned to me rather abruptly and said, "Do you want it? It's yours."

Now when most people make a comment like that, they're joking. You can see it in their face and hear it in their tone. But Mark was serious, and it made me feel more than a tad uncomfortable.

But this was Mark. This was the way he operated.

His kingdom living affected more than finances. It flowed into his posture and his point of view. I had never met anyone who was so laid back. He was never hurried, or rushed, or stressed. In fact, just being around him had a calming effect. My spirit would always feel refreshed after an afternoon with him.

But if I'm honest, part of me felt a little depressed as well. Hanging out with Mark revealed that I often measured myself according to earthly things—things like progress, success, schedules, busyness, achievement. He seemed to measure himself according to *other* things—things like resting in his backyard by the fountain, prayer time with the Father, hosting people around a meal.

John McCollum functions according to kingdom principles too. More than once he blessed me with his generosity. For no apparent reason, he gifted me with some much-needed expertise. I'm not the only one. I've met several others whose lives have been enriched because of John's talents.

But kingdom living goes beyond individuals; it spills into businesses and organizations too. At my church we have a ministry called Grace Clinic. The clinic was conceived by a group of Christians passionate about bringing free health care to people in a nearby area who couldn't afford care. Every Wednesday night doctors, nurses, volunteers, and prayer warriors show up at a place called the Andrews House. One by one the clients come to experience a little taste of the kingdom. We offer them physical care, but we also offer prayer. Some people accept the prayer and others refuse.

A few times the prayer has transitioned from focusing on physical health into a desire for complete wholeness through Jesus Christ. Evidently, when some people get a taste of the kingdom, they want more.

Grace Clinic reminds me of a silly yet profound word picture. The other day I heard a pastor compare followers of Jesus to employees at Baskin-Robbins. If you've ever visited one of these ice cream stores you know about those little pink taster spoons.

It's a simple but brilliant process. You see a flavor that catches your eye. The employee hands you a scoop of that particular ice cream on a little pink spoon. Then it's your call. After tasting, you can walk away. Or you can ask to try something else. Or you can get fifteen scoops of that flavor—just like some people do when they get a taste of the kingdom.

64 King Avenue

Mark Palmer centered his life on living out the kingdom. And he didn't give up on it, even when he looked death right in the eye. The kingdom was his dream because it was Christ's cause. Mark believed it so strongly that many times he invited personal loss rather than abandon a kingdom perspective.

Mark was committed to teach this reality to the Landing Place. He knew it was a critical component of the Transformist life. In March 2003, Mark and Jennifer were in the middle of a series on the kingdom with their Thursday group.

They had just studied Jesus' teaching on revenge and loving your enemies. A member of the Landing Place named Robby led them through some practical ideas on how to be peacemakers in the tradition of Jesus and the early church. Those ideas quickly flowed into a discussion on "two kingdom" theology.

Jesus spoke constantly about the kingdom. It is mentioned over one hundred times in the New Testament and more than fifty times in Matthew's gospel alone. Jesus was asked by the Pharisees when the kingdom would come. He replied, "The kingdom of God is within you" (Luke 17:20–21). For Jesus the kingdom wasn't a future state but rather a present reality.

Because Mark wanted his community to be better citizens of the kingdom, he spoke about it constantly. For him, there were certain people and certain places that made the kingdom seem more of a reality. Mark's regional gatherings, including the last one that he and Jennifer attended three weeks before she passed into the next life, were an example of the kingdom come near.

That particular gathering in Cincinnati was the last time that Jennifer felt okay. On the ride home from that weekend, she felt worse and worse. After the prayer time on that Saturday night, Jennifer came to the conclusion that the earthly healing she wanted so badly was not going to come. She had grown tired of the pain and the fight. She began to transition to the kingdom in its fullness. Both of the Palmers had looked forward to that weekend so much, expecting that God would show up in a powerful way and do something that the Devil would not be able to counteract.

Maybe God did.

For Mark, regional gatherings became what the Celts referred to as a "thin place"—a place where heaven and earth meet. In Mark's language it was a place where the two kingdoms rub against each other, and we're allowed glimpses into that other alternative true reality, the place where Jennifer is now.

Jennifer's death made Mark a mourner. It made him an aching visionary and caused him to feel more acutely the reality of the kingdom, both the "already" and the "not yet." It forced Mark to break all allegiances to this world and its powers and to live more radically in service to the King. Mark saw a direct contrast between the kingdom of heaven and the kingdom of earth. Every follower of Jesus is called to live in light of the reality of the kingdom of heaven. Failing to do so means failing to follow Jesus.

This "kingdom" perspective affects all of life, as shown in the chart.

Component	Kingdom of Earth	Kingdom of Heaven
Core Value	Karma	Grace
Strategy	Life is about advancing my kingdom.	Life is about advancing God's kingdom.
Motivation	Selfish / Evil	Selfless / Good
Response to World	How can others benefit me?	How can I benefit others?
Key Question	How can I use God and others to serve my kingdom?	How can I love God and others to serve his kingdom?
Response to God	God exists to glorify me.	I exist to glorify God.
Concept of Things	I obtain possessions and they end up possessing me.	God gives all things to me as a temporary trust.
Concept of Faith	Poor in faith	Rich in faith
Response to Trials	I must be in control.	God is in control.
Concept of Love	I only love myself.	I love my neighbor as myself.
Response to the Law	Law-breaking	Law-abiding

Component	Kingdom of Earth	Kingdom of Heaven
Relationship to Others	Favoritism / Partiality	Equality / Impartiality
Response to Judging Others	Merciless	Merciful

Figure 13.1: Two Kingdoms

Living according to the rules of the kingdom of heaven sets one apart. It often involves pain, and, honestly, it often *invites* pain. It causes the world to stand up and take notice because it goes against the normal, sometimes unspoken rules of our society. It's the way of the Transformist.

Most believers would rather not accept the kingdom paradox. They'd rather embrace the "not yet." It's much easier because within this mind-set proponents don't have to hope, and, therefore, they don't have to be disappointed.

But Mark never gave up hope. He asked questions, but he knew that not every question could be answered this side of eternity. After intimately knowing cancer's effects on Jennifer and in the midst of cancer consuming his own body, Mark wrote the following in his journal. It provides a window into the Father's kingdom:

> *Thursday, February 17th, 2005, 10:27 pm*
>
> We're all aware of the tension that we live in, the tension of the kingdom, the kingdom come but not in fullness ... the already and the not yet. In the times when we long to see a practical manifestation of the rule and reign of God break into our lives, and yet don't see it, we're tempted to lean towards the side of the "not in its fullness" or the "not yet." My encouragement to you tonight is to lean towards the side of the kingdom come, of the "already." Why not fall towards that? Dare to hope a bit. Give the kingdom come the benefit of the doubt. Take a risk and pray "Your kingdom come" with an air of expectation.

CHAPTER 14

BILINGUAL IS BETTER

If you've ever lived or traveled in the Midwest, you probably know that people in this part of the country get into debates over what to call the nation's favorite beverage. Is it pop, soda, or soda pop?

Trivial? Sure, but not all verbal battles are. Families and friends have split over differences that don't seem much bigger than these. Words can start wars and end them, solve problems and create others. Words heal and words destroy.

John, Kori, Mark, Amy, and Jennifer had a unique way of conversing with the people in their world because their context was unique. Not everyone should "speak" the same way they did. Although loving God and loving people is the only language of relevance, that "language" will sound different because people and circumstances are different.

As Transformists we must not only be able to speak different dialects, we must be bilingual as well. The apostle Paul modeled this for us:

> To the Jews I became like a Jew, to win the Jews. To those under the law I became like one under the law (though I myself am not under the law), so as to win those under the law. To those not

having the law I became like one not having the law (though I am not free from God's law but am under Christ's law), so as to win those not having the law. To the weak I became weak, to win the weak. I have become all things to all [people] so that by all possible means I might save some. I do all this for the sake of the gospel, that I may share in its blessings.

1 Corinthians 9:20–23

Paul didn't adjust who he was, but he did adjust how he communicated. For Transformists, it's critical that we change our methodology without changing our theology.

Presently we're caught between two different mind-sets. Sociologists and anthropologists use different words to explain these two philosophical frameworks, but the most common terms are *modernism* and *postmodernism*. These two terms will pass, certainly. As Transformists, we don't place too much importance on whatever the current era is in which we find ourselves. The point is that we're able to understand the various mind-sets of our age so that we can continue to dialogue with people.

First What, Then Why

Volumes have been written on modernism, postmodernism, and their effect on humanity. We're just going to take a quick peek. We'll start out a little technical, but we'll end up extremely practical. We'll even discover some tools that will help us in our journey toward living life on the fine line.

Modernity—the prevailing Western mind-set of the last few centuries—promoted a monolithic mind-set that believed in underlying universal truths. Knowledge was standardized and considered to be objective, ideal, and absolute. Built in concert with the principles of cause and effect, the scientific method, and authority, modernism acknowledged the existence of fundamental truths in society, culture, and religion. Looking more to institutions than to individuals for answers, modernity's goal was always progress and improvement. Some proponents even believed modernism would make utopia possible, even within the twentieth century.

Certain ads define this period and provide a window into its rationale — ads like "Always Coca-Cola," for example. *Always* suggests a continual, frequent experience. It bucks against individualism. The beverage empire wanted a phrase that communicated a drinking experience that was for *all* people *always.* Another ad slogan that reflects modernism is "Diamonds are forever." Debeers chose "forever" because of its permanence. It suggests unchanging objectivity. Both ads resonate with the promise that modernism offers.

If the claims of modernism were so grandiose, then what caused the change to postmodernism? The answer is fairly simple: people experienced exceptions to the rule. One promise of modernism was that war would end, but the twentieth century proved to be both the most modern and the bloodiest century in human history. Russian author Aleksandr Solzhenitsyn once commented, "The most optimistic century ended as the most cannibalistic."[1]

Modernism also promised that science would solve all of our problems and cure all our diseases, yet the twentieth witnessed the explosion of the AIDS pandemic along with countless other viruses and terminal diseases. Cynicism and skepticism set in, and people began to see more and more deviations from the "universal" rule of objective, ceaseless progress.

A spirit of distrust surfaced — distrust in absolutes, authority, and objectivity. Science and progress weren't the promised saviors. As Friedrich Nietzsche said, "'Progress' is merely a modern idea — that is to say, a false idea."[2] So began postmodernism — a philosophical stance that rejects the absolute claims of modernism and distrusts any system of thought or belief that claims to have all the answers. Postmodern thought encourages people to follow their own truth—their own experience. As Coldplay's Chris Martin, in his song "The Scientist," sings, "Science and progress don't speak as loud as my heart."[3]

Experience has become the new authority within postmodernism—individuals can deconstruct everything and reconstruct it according to their own experience. And so individuals, instead of institutions, have become the authority. We're all main characters in our own small stories, we're authors and interpreters of our own truth.

Postmodernism questions, breaks down, and, in some cases, rejects established standards. But most of all, postmodernism asserts that anyone's ideas, beliefs, and values are worthy of an audience. We aren't told what to think and do by an institution—whether a church or a café—but instead we blaze our own path. An ad that defines this period is Outback Steakhouse's slogan, "No rules. Just right." The entire restaurant experience is about your personal enjoyment in the way that pleases you. The individual, not the institution, is now the arbiter of everything.

Why It's Important

Why is understanding these two different mind-sets so critical in our becoming Transformists? Because all the time, everywhere we go, we're communicating something. The question is not *whether* we're saying something, but rather *what* we're saying and *how* we should say it. Transformists flex the *way* they communicate (not *what* they communicate) based on the other person's location, be it physical, intellectual, emotional, or spiritual.

At Mars Hill, the apostle Paul changed his approach. He knew the Athenians embraced a certain type of mind-set that affected the way they thought, loved, and lived. Paul acknowledged these differences, studied these differences, and communicated his message in a way that resonated with his audience.

The Palmers did this in their context as well. Recognizing that the Short North neighborhood of Columbus, Ohio, was a part of the city saturated with artists, ideas, creativity, and caring for the environment, they were intentional about doing life and church differently in a way that spoke to their culture.

As Transformists, when relating with our world, it's critical that we model Paul's example to the Athenians. We too must acknowledge people's differences, study these differences, and then communicate our lives in a way that resonates with our audience.

What are some of these differences?

Component	Modernism	Postmodernism
Motto	Tell me	Involve me
Learning Style	Lecture	Story
Value	Truth	Tolerance
Concept of Salvation	A point in time	A way of life
Concept of Truth	The Bible, the whole Bible, and nothing but the Bible	All truth is God's truth
Tendency of Extreme	Legalism	Liberalism
Order of Worship	Fixed	Fluid
Concept of Church	We do church	We are church
Interpretation of the Bible	Literal, historical, grammatical	Communal
Concept of Authority	Hierarchy	Roundtable
Camp of Choice	Separatist	Conformist

Figure 14.1: Modernism and Postmodernism

How do you feel when reading this chart?

I feel torn. For much of my life I naturally resonated with the "modernism" side of the chart. I grew up believing that we "do" church and that the Bible was the only place God revealed truth. Yet in recent years I've realized that, as God's people, we "are" the church, and although the Bible is the Truth, God has deposited truth all over his beautiful creation if we just have the eyes to see it.

Irrelevant Extremes

The people we interact with on a daily basis lean toward one of these two mind-sets, just like we do. Churches aren't exempt from these mind-sets either. They typically take on the personality of one of them.

So if Separatists gravitate toward modernism and Conformists toward postmodernism, where do Transformists' loyalties lie?

Transformists transcend these categories of cultural phenomena. Transformists walk the fine line between modernism and postmodernism. At times, they pull from both perspectives, since both have valid points. Yet Transformists don't get sucked into one of these systems because systems come and go; eras have expiration dates.

Walking this fine line is a heap of work that never ends. It's a moment-by-moment process of dependence upon Jesus. Maybe this is why so few people are willing to take the step toward the fine line.

How does someone walk the fine line between modernism and postmodernism?

Take the component of biblical interpretation for a moment. The modernist views biblical interpretation as something cerebral, passive, and external. People dissect passages much like scientists dissect specimens in a laboratory. Their tendency is to remove themselves from the process, merely reading the Bible instead of the Bible also reading them. The scientist performs an experiment. The student performs analysis. Application is often absent. The text is something merely to be uncovered, excavated, and brought under the interpreter's control.

The postmodern loyalists determine the meaning of a text by discovering what it means to them. They invite their community to interpret the Scripture in light of their experience. Turning a blind eye to historical context, cultural ramifications, and rules of grammar, their entire process is relative and subjective. Postmodernists make themselves the center of the hermeneutical universe and ignore centuries of sound biblical exegesis. Columbus-area pastor Aric Birdsell provides an explanation: "That's where we get our truth from, from our experience, from what works, what we have felt instead of A plus B equals C."[4]

Transformists don't swing to either side. They incorporate both perspectives. They utilize solid exegetical methods by examining the historical background, the genre (poetry, prophecy, etc.), and the word usage of a particular passage. In this entire process they submit themselves to the Holy Spirit and seek God, not an experience. But in seeking God, many times they have an experience.

Transformists work out their theology within their communities of faith. They don't stop at just reading the Bible, they allow the Bible to read them too by always asking the Holy Spirit to reveal areas in their lives that fall short of God's ideal. They make the necessary adjustments in the areas of their lives that don't measure up. For them, part of the interpretation process includes asking, "What does it mean for us to apply this passage in our lives?"

They don't stop at merely understanding the Scriptures, they embody them.

Can You Hear Me Now?

The normal human tendency is that we communicate in only one way. It's been said that we don't hear things the way they are, we hear them the way we are. When we refuse to become bilingual, to speak in the language of our listeners, we force others to adjust to us, our preferences, and our way of approaching life. This isn't the way of Christ.

Jesus understood the fine line.

He didn't compromise, but he did allow himself to be inconvenienced as he adjusted to our needs and our way of communicating. Jesus laid aside his rights and privileges so that we might understand him and the hope he offers. He spoke relevantly, and he invites us to model his example.

This is what makes the Transformist camp so exciting — we have the privilege of asking ourselves how we can better communicate God's love in our current context. Remember the quote from chapter 1? How Christ is relevant to the world in which we live now is "arguably the most basic ethical question of the Christian faith."[5]

Transformists embrace every opportunity to answer this ethical question. How can we best present Christ in a world that desperately needs to hear the healing language of love in words it understands? Are we speaking love to a hurting world?

If not, what are we afraid of?

PART V

THE FINE LINE

Do not fear death so much,
but rather the inadequate life.
Bertolt Brecht

CHAPTER 15

AFRAID OF WHAT?

For a hundred reasons, I love the movie *What about Bob?*

Bill Murray plays Bob Wiley, a multiphobic obsessive-compulsive patient who crashes the family vacation of an egotistical psychiatrist, Dr. Leo Marvin, played by Richard Dreyfuss.

In one scene, we find Bob sleeping over at the Marvins' house because of a violent thunderstorm. With few beds available, Bob ends up staying in the room of the son, Sigmund. Sigmund is a young boy whose life is paralyzed by fear—he won't even dive off the pier into the lake, which drives his father crazy. With thunder crashing, Sigmund and Bob have a man-to-man talk about fear:

> *Sigmund*: Are you afraid of death?
> *Bob*: Yeah.
> *Sigmund*: Me too. There's no way out of it. You're going to die. I'm going to die. It's going to happen. What difference does it make if it's tomorrow or in years? I'm going to die! You are going to die.
> *Bob*: Then there's nothing to be afraid of.
> *Sigmund*: Well, not diving anymore.[1]

Although cast humorously in the movie, fear truly is the great equalizer. Fear is found in every culture, and no one is immune from it, not even Transformists. Author and anthropologist Donald Brown, in his book *Human Universals*, suggests that every society has five common fears.[2] These five fears threaten our ability to be Transformists. They're obstacles to living life on the fine line. Understanding these fears and pushing through them is a critical step in achieving a life of relevance.

The Fab Five

Fear of Death (Our Own Death and the Death of Our Family)

Explanation: People in every society want to protect themselves and their children. They want security, and they take self-preservation seriously. Although they might define it differently, nearly every culture prohibits murder and suicide and incorporates contempt for these behaviors. We're taught from a young age to safeguard our livelihood.

Application: Transformists must expect to die. This death may be a literal cessation of life, but more often it's not. It may mean that we must kill our prejudice, our need for security, or our own pride.

Should we be surprised? Death is the message of Jesus. He said, "If anyone would come after me, he must deny himself and take up his cross daily and follow me" (Luke 9:23). Death is a daily event that includes the big things as well as the little ones.

I was on a plane trying to finish a writing deadline, but had to let my own desires die. I knew God would have me share life with the person in the next seat. In exchange for my little "death," I met Jeremy, a pediatrician doing his residency in Louisville. I learned that he is single and loves physics. He went to a Baptist school as a child and is a fan of Pastor John Piper's books. We chatted for an hour and a half. I wouldn't know any of this without dying that small death that day.

How does this help me walk the fine line? A critical step in living as a Transformist is to love people. The only way I can love people is to get to know people. I may not ever see Jeremy again, and I don't know what will come of meeting him, but that's not my responsibility. As a Transformist, I'm just called to obey. The results are always up to God.

Fear of the Outsider

Explanation: Every society has a set definition of what it means to belong, and, from an early age, society warns people to avoid strangers. Because of this, even the youngest members of society establish rules that govern their groups and cliques. Other children are expected to embrace these rules if they want to be invited in. Our need for community is so strong that at times we'll do things we normally wouldn't do just to blend in.

Application: As we examined earlier, the Separatist and Conformist camps have certain rules that members must keep in order to maintain their insider status. But the price for embracing these rules is irrelevance.

Every Transformist moves to an outsider status for rejecting the established rules of the Separatist and Conformist camps. These camps view Transformists as Judas figures—betrayers and black sheep. If Separatists or Conformists were to accept Transformists, that would mean they must also change, something they're against. And so they erect walls and throw stones.

Transformists, however, would rather be relevant than popular. Their desire to please God is stronger than their desire to please others. Paul concluded, "Am I now trying to win human approval, or God's approval? Or am I trying to please people? If I were still trying to please people, I would not be a servant of Christ" (Galatians 1:10 TNIV).

Fear of the Future

Explanation: Every society understands the idea of future. They have words that paint the future with good fortune—words like *hope, optimism, anticipation*. Since the beginning of time, societies have honored people who promise to predict the future, people like fortune-tellers or economists. By knowing what's going to happen ahead of time, we're able to obtain a coveted commodity: control.

Application: Although Separatists and Conformists don't know the future, their irrelevant systems give them the illusion that they do. Separatists reject all things, and Conformists accept all things. Thinking they love God, Separatists declare their loyalty to Christianity. Thinking they love people, Conformists declare their loyalty to culture. Consumed with control, both camps are just two sides of the same irrelevant coin.

Transformists accept the reality that they're not in control. They don't know the future any more than Separatists or Conformists, but the difference is they're not afraid to admit it. Embracing adventure, Transformists recognize the great privilege they have in being part of God's story rather than trying to write their own. They trust in a Person rather than a system or set of rules. They place their future in the hands of the One who holds it anyway. "I make known the end from the beginning, from ancient times, what is still to come. I say: My purpose will stand, and I will do all that I please" (Isaiah 46:10).

Fear of Chaos

Explanation: Every society has a story about how the world came to be, and each one presents a world created out of chaos. Christianity is no exception. The Scriptures say the "earth was formless and empty" (Genesis 1:2). The English word *formless* is translated from the Hebrew word *tohu*, meaning chaos and confusion. Such was the state of the world until God stepped in, and such is the state of our lives until God steps in.

Application: Transformists don't avoid uncertainty; in fact they embrace it. True transformation demands it. University of Michigan professor Robert E. Quinn explains, "Deep change means surrendering control. Making a deep change involves abandoning and 'walking into the land of uncertainty.'"[3]

Transformists recognize that life on the fine line is unpredictable. There are no formulas and no guarantees.

This is the beauty of Transformists: they actually depend upon God. They must depend on him because loving God and people looks different in different circumstances. There are no prepackaged answers. Transformists boldly step out into the unknown, following Jesus because only he knows the way. "Let us fix our eyes on Jesus, the author and perfecter of our faith" (Hebrews 12:2).

Fear of Insignificance

Explanation: Despite the fact that societies function in terms of what's best for the group, every society also acknowledges the individual, having a word for self-image and recognizing that self-esteem is somewhat dependent on other people's perceptions of us. Whether we like to admit it or not, on differing levels we crave the respect of others and greatly fear their indifference toward us.

Application: Transformists aren't enslaved by other people's opinions. They're content to walk the fine line even though sometimes it's a lonely place. Not so with Separatists and Conformists. They want the affirmation of others, and so they're not willing to abandon their irrelevant camps.

Like everyone else, Transformists want to make their mark on the world. However, unlike everyone else, they actually do. Although Separatists and Conformists show glimmers of hope, the pressures to separate from the world or conform to it are too great. They figure there's just too much to lose. Transformists aren't afraid to lose. "For whoever wants to save his life will lose it, but whoever loses his life for me and for the gospel will save it" (Mark 8:35).

Transformists never reach a place where they eradicate their fears; instead they transcend them. When I think of a Transformist who overcame his fears with love, I think of Mark Palmer. Below is one of his journal entries. Keep in mind it was written before the battle with Jennifer's cancer:

Wednesday, February 19th, 2003 11:07am
A long while ago my friend Joe Boyd from Vegas posted this on his journal, and I then posted it on mine. I rediscovered it in my paper journal last night, and it deserves a reposting. It continues to be an encouragement to me when I get beat up for doing what God has called me to do.

Expect pain.

Expect to be misunderstood.

Expect to be persecuted and expect it to come first from those who follow Jesus.

Expect to be maligned, attacked, and ridiculed from all sides.

Expect to grow tired and weary.

Expect to want to give up.

Expect to lose many old friends. Expect to lose all of your friends where the "church" is the central reason for your friendship. Only your deep and Christ-centered friendships will endure.

Expect to be labeled (a freak, a hippie, a cult leader, a quitter, a fraud, an idealist, a purist, a heretic, a divider, a communist, a jerk, an egomaniac, a devil worshiper). Yes, I've been called them all to my face.

Expect to weep ... deeper and stronger than you ever have.

Expect to doubt your calling, your convictions, your path, your faith, and your life.

Expect to be lonely.

Expect to be seen as utterly unsuccessful.

Expect to die … nothing will be left of you. You will cease to exist. The last things in you to die will be your desire to be great for God and your desire to be happy. And then, you will finally …

Live. Expect life. Expect meaning. Expect to finally understand the prophets and apostles. Expect to know Jesus and his life … for that is all that you will have … and that is all that you need.

The Transformist Credo

In my seasons of walking the fine line, I've met some fascinating followers of Jesus. I've been inspired by their freedom and liberated by their courage. Spending time in the Transformist camp, I've picked up on some patterns. Here are some of those findings:

As Transformists we don't need to have everything figured out, for that would mean we're Separatists. We don't need to say anything goes, for that would mean we're Conformists. We neither add to God's Word nor do we ignore it. Instead, we obey it.

We're not perfect, but we're seekers. We long to have a pure relationship with the Creator of the universe. We desire to know the "why" behind the "what" and the purpose behind the principle. Of course there will be mistakes along the way, but this is what sets us apart. We have a little more grace and patience with each other because we know what we've been saved from.

The movement is beginning. The gathering has united. We come from a variety of backgrounds, but we share a common purpose. Above all else, we passionately love God and people. We don't fear culture because we're called to shape it. We don't fear Christianity because we're called to embody it. We are the relevant. We are the Transformists.

Hanging Up

Even though this book is about to end, the conversation doesn't have to. Living life on the fine line is a beautiful mess. It's where we work out our salvation, and it stops only when we stop thinking, dreaming, and re-envisioning.

In the introduction I invited you into an honest dialogue. I invited you to pick up the phone. But now it's time to hang up and live it out. This reminds me of another scene from *The Matrix*. Neo finally discovered the truth and embraced who he was born to be. The movie ends with Neo dialoguing on the phone. Let's listen in on his conversation:

> I know you're out there. I can feel you now. I know that you're afraid ... you're afraid of us. You're afraid of change. I don't know the future. I didn't come here to tell you how this is going to end. I came here to tell you how it's going to begin. I'm going to hang up this phone, and then I'm going to show these people what you don't want them to see. I'm going to show them a world without you. A world without rules and controls, without borders or boundaries. A world where anything is possible. Where we go from there is a choice I leave to you.[4]

So how will it all go down after we hang up, you ask?
That's entirely up to you.

DISCUSSION QUESTIONS

INTRODUCTION: The Phone Is Ringing

1. Why do you think the song "Losing My Religion" resonated with an entire generation?

2. In your mind, is it a good thing or a bad thing to "lose your religion"? Why?

3. Do you feel like you have found your "place in this world"? If so, how did that happen? If not, what do you think it will take?

4. If you attend church, what do you usually feel when you attend? Why?

5. Discuss how your friends and family celebrate or suppress mystery.

CHAPTER 1: Walking the Line

1. Do you agree with this statement: How Christ is relevant to the world in which we live now is "arguably the most basic ethical question of the Christian faith." Why or why not?

2. Why do you think many young adults leave the church during their late teens and twenties?

3. Do the majority of the people you know live as people *out* of the world or as people *of* the world?

4. How have Christians tried to live *in* the world yet not be *of* it? Has it worked?

5. What daily tensions might you experience if you're committed to both your culture and your Christianity?

CHAPTER 2: Divided We Fall

1. How have you seen the church at war with itself?

2. Which camp, the Separatists or the Conformists, has been a bigger influence on your life? Why?

3. What are some of the key divisive issues between the Separatists and the Conformists?

4. What are the consequences when the church is divided?

5. Why are these three questions (Where are we? What should we do? How do we do it?) critical to discovering how to live on the fine line?

CHAPTER 3: Under the Sun

1. How do you see the Eden story: as a cruel setup or a generous gift? What does your answer say about your tendencies toward Separatism?

2. What are some ways that you rationalize sin within your own life?

3. In what ways have you added to God's Word? Can you think of any specific "commands" that you've added to your Christianity?

4. Are you more likely to view culture as a friend or an enemy? Why?

5. What makes Separatists and Conformists irrelevant?

CHAPTER 4: The Ancient Donkey

1. Why is it hard for us to know when we're being relevant?

2. What do most people equate relevance with? Have you ever been guilty of this? What should we equate relevance with?

3. What group of people is closest to God's heart? Are they closest to yours?

4. What are some ways you've spoken the language of relevance to those in your world?

5. What are some practical steps you can take to get off your "donkey"?

CHAPTER 5: The Spiritual Aspirin

1. As you look at the Worldview Comparison (figure 5.2), which side of the chart best describes you? Are there any areas you'd like to change? Why?

2. What are the dangers of viewing only professional ministers as priests? How does your answer affect your everyday life?

3. What's so symbolic about the fulcrum? Describe one person who embodied relevance to you. What made the individual memorable?

4. Have you ever met someone wounded by an irrelevant Christian? Please share the scenario if you're comfortable discussing it.

5. As you think about the life of Jesus, what story or situation impacts you the most?

CHAPTER 6: Fifty-Foot Column

1. Although living atop a column may seem ridiculous, what are some other common examples of Separatists attempting to leave the world?

2. Are personal convictions bad in and of themselves? Why or why not?

3. What are the three characteristics of a Separatist, and which do you struggle with the most? Why?

4. What is the motivating factor of a Separatist? Is this a surprise? Why or why not?

5. Why is it dangerous to depend upon other people's personal convictions?

CHAPTER 7: The Girl Bashers

1. If you have angst regarding the church, what should you do about it?

2. What are the three characteristics of a Conformist, and which do you struggle with most? Why?

3. What's behind Conformists functioning as chameleons of culture? Is this ever true about your life? If so, how?

4. What's missing from the church when you're missing? Please spend time telling someone in your group what they uniquely contribute to the body of Christ.

5. What's the difference between forms and functions? What forms need to change in your life or church? Why?

CHAPTER 8: Orange Construction Cones

1. What is it about orange construction cones that make Separatists and Conformists prefer them?

2. What's your view of change? Do you like it in your own life? Why or why not?

3. Depending on where you are in the process, share some thoughts on how God drew you, or is beginning to draw you, away from the Separatist or Conformist camps.

4. Do you consider yourself to be more a student of the Word or a student of the world? What evidence do you have for your answer?

5. What are the places in your world, like Mars Hill, where ideas, philosophies, and religions are shared? What's stopping you from showing up there as a Transformist?

CHAPTER 9: Skin-Deep Love

1. Why is it so important for us to love God in a connected way?

2. What are some of your observations about the story of David and the ark? How do these observations relate to your life?

3. Do you believe God is safe? Do you believe God is good? Why or why not?

4. Why does our love for God grow only when our need for him grows? Please give some illustrations.

5. Do you see yourself as spiritually bankrupt? Why or why not?

CHAPTER 10: Position Is Everything

1. Do you love yourself the wrong way? Why or why not?

2. What motivated ascetics to engage in their dark acts? Do you believe they loved themselves the wrong way? Does asceticism appeal to you at all?

3. Which ABCs of your condition roll around in your head? How often do you dwell on these phrases? How do you think they affect how you see yourself?

4. Which ABCs of your position speak to your heart in a special way? How often do you dwell on these phrases? How do you think they affect how you see yourself?

5. If we want to be relevant, why is it so critical that we view ourselves and love ourselves the way God does? What one thing will enable us to do that?

CHAPTER 11: Perfect Blue Buildings

1. What people or places in your world don't look like they have much potential? What could God do in and through you for these people and places?

2. As a Transformist, how important is it for you to see and hear other people's stories? How did John McCollum model that? How can you improve in that area?

3. What resources do you have that you could use to serve others and meet their needs?

4. Respond to François-René de Chateaubriand's quote. How is your life compartmentalized? How is it interconnected?

5. What about the McCollums' story impacted you? What about their story can you take and apply within your own life?

CHAPTER 12: Angels Do Exist

1. As you read about Jennifer's death, what questions surfaced in your own heart? Do you feel like you can ask those questions of God?

2. Respond to the list of five things that angered Mark.

3. What strikes you about the way Mark viewed community? Do you agree with it? What would have to change in order for you to model this in your own life?

4. Mark loved God with his mind. Does this characterize your life? What's one practical thing you can do in order to make this more of a reality?

5. What questions surface when reading about Mark's last moments? What about Mark's and Amy's lives spoke to you the loudest?

CHAPTER 13: Thy Kingdom Come

1. Do you think Jesus' Sermon on the Mount is for Christians today? Why or why not?

2. What are some specific ways the world would change if followers of Christ lived out chapters 5–7 of Matthew's gospel?

3. Have you met anyone who lived his or her life according to kingdom principles? How were those principles manifested here on earth?

4. In what ways have you recently passed out "little pink spoon" samples of the kingdom? What was the response?

5. When comparing the two kingdoms (figure 13.1), what sticks out to you? Which component is easiest for you? Which is hardest? Why?

CHAPTER 14: Bilingual Is Better

1. How does modernism appeal to a Christian? Postmodernism? How might modernism be unappealing to a Christian? Postmodernism?

2. Why is modernism so appealing to the world and culture? Postmodernism?

3. Why is it so important for Transformists to understand the mindset of different people? And why is it so important that we change the way we communicate with the world when it comes to sharing our faith in Jesus?

4. Looking at modernism and postmodernism (figure 14.1), on which side of the chart do you often find yourself? Is this a good thing or a bad thing? Why?

5. Think of a specific situation in your life right now that you're wrestling with. What would it look like for you to be a Transformist in that situation? How is that different from what you're doing?

CHAPTER 15: Afraid of What?

1. What has to die in order for you to become or to remain a Transformist?

2. How does the desire to be an insider keep you from relevance? How can you transcend this fear?

3. What's your biggest fear about the future? Does your answer provide any insight regarding your relationship with God?

4. What mark do you want to leave on the world? What are you willing to sacrifice in order to achieve it?

5. As you read the final journal entry from Mark Palmer, what emotions do you feel? What thoughts do you think? Are you ready and willing to walk the fine line? Why or why not?

MODERNISM AND POSTMODERNISM COMPARISON

Motto

Modernism = Tell me
They would rather have the experts tell them the facts.

Postmodernism = Involve me
They would rather experience and judge for themselves.

Learning Style

Modernism = Lecture
They enjoy a systematic breakdown of a subject matter.

Postmodernism = Story
They enjoy hearing people paint pictures with words.

Value

Modernism = Truth
They place a high priority on the reality of situations and
circumstances.

Postmodernism = Tolerance
They place a high value on hearing others and what they
bring to the table.

Concept of Salvation

Modernism = A point in time
They tend to emphasize the initial profession of faith in
Jesus in order to escape an eternity in hell. They focus on
how Jesus desires to change our eternal destiny.

Postmodernism = A way of life
They tend to emphasize the journey of faith in terms of
its holistic effect on all of life. They focus on how Jesus
desires to change our world.

Concept of Truth

Modernism = The Bible, the whole Bible, and nothing but the Bible
They believe God shows up solely in his Word.

Postmodernism = All Truth is God's Truth
They believe God shows up all over the place, not just in the
Bible, and it's our job to discover when, where, and how.

Tendency of Extreme

Modernism = Legalism
> They are unbalanced in their loyalties to rules and regulations.

Postmodernism = Liberalism
> They are unbalanced in their loyalties to acceptance and accommodation.

Order of Worship

Modernism = Fixed
> They place a high priority upon order, tradition, and predictability within their gatherings.

Postmodernism = Fluid
> They place a high priority upon flexibility, creativity, and participation within their gatherings.

Concept of Church

Modernism = We do church
> They see church as something we attend.

Postmodernism = We are church
> They see the church as something we embody.

Interpretation of the Bible

Modernism = Literal, Historical, Grammatical
They interpret the Bible in light of its genre, tradition, and word usage.

Postmodernism = Communal
They interpret the Bible in light of how it affects the community of faith.

Concept of Authority

Modernism = Hierarchy
They posture their leadership around people's calling, gifting, and position.

Postmodernism = Roundtable
They posture their leadership around people's impressions, suggestions, and input.

Camp of Choice

Modernism = Separatist
Their loyalties lie with the Separatist camp.

Postmodernism = Conformist
Their loyalties lie with the Conformist camp.

NOTES

A Note to the Reader

1. John G. Stackhouse Jr., professor of theology and culture, Regent College. Editor, *No Other Gods Before Me?Evangelicals and the Challenge of World Religions* (Grand Rapids, Mich.: Baker, 2001).

CHAPTER 1: Walking the Line

1. Michael Joseph Gross, a journalist and author of *Star Struck*, in a review on *www.amazon.com*.

2. David Kinnaman, "Twentysomethings Struggle to Find Their Place in Christian Churches." Posted September 24, 2003. *The Barna Group*: *www.barna .org/FlexPage.aspx?Page=BarnaUpdate&BarnaUpdateID=149* (August 30, 2007).

CHAPTER 2: Divided We Fall

1. Abraham Lincoln, "Lincoln's 'House Divided' speech." *PBS*: *www.pbs.org /wgbh/aia/part4/4h2934t.html* (August 14, 2008).

CHAPTER 4: The Ancient Donkey

1. "Relevant." *Merriam-Webster's Dictionary of Law*: *www.dictionary.reference. com/browse/relevant* (July 8, 2008).

2. Frank E. Hirsch, *International Standard Bible Encyclopedia* (Grand Rapids, Mich.: Eerdmans, 1939), available on CD-ROM.

3. Bob Deffinbaugh, "The Good Samaritan." *Bible.org*: *www.bible.org/page .php?page_id=1104* (August 30, 2007).

4. "The community is to have the same rules for you and for the alien living among you; this is a lasting ordinance for the generations to come. You and the alien shall be the same before the LORD. The same laws and regulations will apply both to you and to the alien living among you" (Numbers 15:15–16).

CHAPTER 5: The Spiritual Aspirin

1. James Bratt, *Abraham Kuyper: A Centennial Reader* (Grand Rapids, Mich.: Eerdmans, 1998), 488.

2. Bill Thrall, Bruce McNicol, and Ken McElrath, *The Ascent of a Leader* (San Francisco: Jossey-Bass, 1999), 101–2.

3. Craig R. Thompson, ed. and trans., *The Colloquies of Erasmus* (Chicago: University of Chicago Press, 1965), 630.

4. Mahmoud A. El-Gamal, *Islamic Finance: Law, Economics, and Practice* (Cambridge, Mass.: Cambridge University Press, 2006), 1.

5. Of course, by "every vocation," I am referring to those that are in accordance with moral and civil law.

6. Marvin R. Wilson, *Our Father Abraham* (Grand Rapids, Mich.: Eerdmans, 1989), 177.

CHAPTER 6: Fifty-Foot Column

1. "In Pictures: Magician's pillar marathon." Posted May 23, 2002. *BBC News World Edition*: *news.bbc.co.uk/2/hi/entertainment/2004046.stm* (September 15, 2007).

2. Herbert Thurston, transcribed by Robert B. Olson, "St. Simeon Stylites the Elder." *New Advent*: *www.newadvent.org/cathen/13795a.htm* (September 12, 2007).

3. Tracey R. Rich. *Judaism 101*: *www.jewfaq.org/613.htm* (August 30, 2007).

4. Robert F. McNamara, "Simeon Stylite." *Saints Alive*: *www. irondequoitcatholic.org/index.php/St/SimeonStylite* (September 13, 2007).

5. PBS, *Frontline*: *http://www.pbs.org/wgbh/pages/frontline/shows/jesus/ interviews/wallis.html* (August 10, 2008).

6. As humans, we all come to the Bible with preconceived biases. When we approach the Word, we need to invite the Holy Spirit to give us God's view on the issues at hand.

7. "Homiletics Interview: Kenneth L. Woodward," *Homiletics online*: *www .homileticsonline.com/subscriber/interviews/woodward.asp* (July 8, 2008).

8. Dan Buck, "Getting Out of the Faith Ghetto," *www.danbuckblogspot.com* (July 8, 2008).

9. *Les Misérables*, DVD, directed by Billie August, writers Victor Hugo, Rafael Yglesias. *Les Miserables* script, *Dialogue Transcript*: *www.script-o-rama.com/movie _scripts/l/les-miserables-script-transcript-hugo.html* (1998).

CHAPTER 7: The Girl Bashers

1. Dan Kimball, *Vintage Faith*: *dankimball.typepad.com/vintage_faith/2005/03 /moby_and_christ.html* (October 26, 2007).

2. *Google Answers*: *www.answers.google.com/answers/threadview?id=56750* (November 7, 2005).

3. A = "not." Muse = "think." Amuse = "to not think."

4. Stephen Ryan, "Chaplains Are More Than What Chaplains Do." *National Association of Catholic Chaplains*: *www.nacc.org/vision/articles/chaplains-are-more. asp* (September 20, 2007); Terry Gips, "The Natural Step's Fourth Condition for Sustainability and Manfred Max-Neef's Basic Needs Analysis," *The Alliance for Sustainability*: *homepages.mtn.org/iasa/tgmaxneef.html* (September 20, 2007).

5. "Your words have helped the tottering to stand, And you have strengthened feeble knees" (Job 4:4 NASB).

6. Ambrose Redmoon. *Quoteland.com*: *www.quoteland.com/author. asp?AUTHOR_ID=110* (July 14, 2008).

7. "The Lord GOD has given Me the tongue of disciples, That I may know how to sustain the weary one with a word. He awakens Me morning by morning, He awakens My ear to listen as a disciple" (Isaiah 50:4 NASB).

8. A. W. Tozer, *The Knowledge of the Holy* (San Francisco: HarperSanFrancisco, 1978), 3.

9. Genesis 4:3–5; 1 Samuel 15:19–23; Leviticus 10:1–2.

10. Tozer, *Knowledge of the Holy*, 8.

11. Gordon MacKenzie, *Orbiting the Giant Hairball: A Corporate Fool's Guide to Surviving with Grace* (New York: Penguin, 1996), 19.

12. Gene A. Getz, *Elders and Leaders: God's Plan for Leading the Church* (Chicago: Moody, 2003), 36.

13. Ibid., 37.

CHAPTER 8: Orange Construction Cones

1. Acts 22:3.

2. Matthew G. Easton and Paul S. Taylor, "Paul." *Bible Encyclopedia*: *www .christiananswers.net/dictionary/paul.html* (September 25, 2007).

3. John MacArthur, *Galatians: The Wondrous Grace of God* (Nashville: Nelson, 2000), 17.

4. Strabo, *Geographica*, vol. 14:5, 13.

5. William M. Ramsay, *The Cities of St. Paul: Their Influence on His Life and Thought* (London: Hodder & Stoughton, 1907), 179.

6. "Athens." *Easton's Bible Dictionary: www.sacred-texts.com/bib/ebd/ebd036.htm* (September 27, 2007).

7. Greg Herrick, "Is the Bible the Only Revelation from God?" *Bible.org: www.bible.org/page.php?page_id=678* (September 27, 2007). Epimenides' quote is taken from his poem *Cretica*. Aratus's quote is taken from *Phaenonlena 5*, "It is with Zeus that every one of us in every way has to do, for we are also his offspring." It had appeared earlier in Cleanthes's "Hymn to Zeus." See also "2nd Missionary Journey: Athens." *The Boston Christian Bible Study Resources: www .bcbsr.com/books/acts17b.html* (September 27, 2007).

8. Joseph Stiglmayr, transcribed by Geoffrey K. Mondello, "Dionysius the Pseudo-Areopagite." *Catholic Encyclopedia: www.newadvent.org/cathen/05013a.htm* (September 27, 2007).

9. "2nd Missionary Journey." *Boston Christian Bible Study Resources: www.bcbsr .com/books/acts17b.html* (September 27, 2007).

CHAPTER 9: Skin-Deep Love

1. The conversation of how many parts make up a person is significant and relevant in many aspects of theological study. But in regard to our conversation of how to be in the world but not be of it, the significant point is how the different parts of a person connect and relate in one's holistic love for God. It's impossible to be relevant when you love God with only a part of yourself rather than your whole self. A disconnected love for God is theologically incorrect and detrimental to maintaining the life of a Transformist.

Additional sources are listed here for the reader who desires to study more about the specific parts that make up an individual: See Gordon H. Clark, *The Biblical Doctrine of Man* (Unicoi, Tenn.: Trinity Foundation, 1984); Lewis S. Chafer, *Systematic Theology* (Dallas: Dallas Seminary Press, 1947); William H. Baker, "Lesson 5," *Survey of Theology II* (Chicago: Moody Bible Institute, 1990).

2. When coupled with "love your neighbor as yourself (Matthew 22:35–40).

3. John B. Woodward, "Theological Models of Man's Makeup," *Man as Spirit, Soul, and Body. Grace Notebook: www.gracenotebook.biblemessages.com/pub/87* (May 19, 2008).

CHAPTER 10: Position Is Everything

1. Alexander Whyte, *Bunyan Characters in the Pilgrim's Progress* (London: Oliphant Anderson and Ferrier, 1903), 98.

CHAPTER 11: Perfect Blue Buildings

1. David J. Drucker, "Defining Success." Posted June 2007. *Financial Advisor Magazine: www.fa-mag.com/past_issues.php?id=1500&idPastIssue=122* (July 11, 2008).

CHAPTER 12: Angels Do Exist

1. Mark Palmer described this final gathering in his journal and included these words from the singing, in part from the Lord's Prayer, Matthew 6:9–10.

2. "Testing the Strong Ones," lyrics by Aaron Marsh, Copeland, © 2003. Reprint by permission.

CHAPTER 13: Thy Kingdom Come

1. Bill Somers, *Essay on the Kingdom of God: www.etpv.org/bills_page/essay.html* (October 22, 2007).

CHAPTER 14: Bilingual Is Better

1. Tim Chester, *Justice, Mercy, and Humility* (Carlisle, U.K.: Paternoster, 2003).

2. Friedrich Nietzsche, *The Antichrist* (Sioux Falls, S.D.: NuVision, 2007), 4.

3. "The Scientist," lyrics by Coldplay, *A Rush of Blood to the Head* (2002).

4. Dennis M. Mahoney, "Where Seekers Gather," *Columbus Dispatch* (November 12, 2004).

5. Michael Joseph Gross, a journalist and author of *Star Struck*, in a review on *www.amazon.com*.

CHAPTER 15: Afraid of What?

1. *What about Bob?* (Hollywood: Touchstone Pictures, 1991).

2. Donald E. Brown, *Human Universals* (Philadelphia: Temple University Press, 1991).

3. Robert E. Quinn, *Deep Change* (San Francisco: Jossey-Bass, 1996), 3–4.

4. "Memorable quotes for *The Matrix*." *The Internet Movie Database: www.imdb .com/title/tt0133093/quotes* (October 21, 2007).

LIST OF FIGURES

ACKNOWLEDGMENTS

It is amazing what you can accomplish
if you do not care who gets the credit.
Harry Truman

Credit.

It's a funny word.

Some of us live on it regularly—not having enough for today, we borrow from tomorrow. Counting on the future, we promise to pay back the present.

Here are a few who have lent me a bit of their future. I wish I could give them more credit, but this will have to do. Obviously I'm indebted ...

Kelly, you've given me the gift of patience because we both know my imperfections. I love you and your strengths, which so often bring balance to my weaknesses.

Redeem the Day Advisory Board members (David Coleman, Ron Kuck, Jeff Martin, and Peter Pavarini), your wisdom is invaluable.

Angela Scheff, for understanding the need for this book (even before it was written) and for making my writing sharper and stronger.

Marcy Schorsch, your belief in me has opened many doors.

John and Kate Ward (*drawproductions.com*), two fellow risk-takers, it's always refreshing to partner with you.

Brian Rants (*eye9design.com*), you're a dreamer who has supported my insanity since the beginning.

Josh Franer, the Picasso of film, I'm constantly amazed by your artistic eye.

Chet Scott, who introduced me to Roger Hall, who introduced me to Zondervan.

Kasey Ingram and S. James Turoff, your counsel gave me confidence in this process.

Gabe Taviano (*taviano.com*), you're a creative genius who invests in the kingdom.

My colleagues: Mark Artrip, Tim Farner, Dustin Godshall, Rick Nuzum, Sean Spoelstra, and Phil Stoll—where should I start? It's never dull.

And to a few of those who take care of my soul and love me unconditionally: Nate Harrison, Matt Reid, Mike Myers, and Gary Underwood.